The Wine Country of France

The
Wine Country
of France

EDWARD HYAMS

J. B. Lippincott Company
PHILADELPHIA & NEW YORK
1960

CONTENTS

FOREWORD

THERE are numerous books in English about the great wines of France by people who know a great deal more about them than I do. I have tried only to say something about the origins of the vineyards and their geography from the holiday-maker's point of view; those I know I have discussed, those I do not I have only mentioned. To the great wines, therefore, this book is an introduction and sometimes an explanation; it is not a connoisseur's appreciation and it is intended for, as it were, beginners.

The lesser but still exquisite wines of France have been rather neglected in favour of the great ones. I have tried therefore to give as much or even more attention to them, for they deserve it. Moreover, in every case, they are grown in country far pleasanter and more interesting than the three regions which are most famous for great wines. For the Englishman who is fond of wine, interested in wine, but cannot distinguish one famous claret from another or even be quite certain of telling a Bordeaux from a Burgundy, there is perhaps more pleasure to be found in discovering a delicious wine he has never heard of in Lorraine, on the Loire, up the Dordogne, or in the Jura, than in being the millionth respectful amateur to confirm the not-always-disinterested specialist's opinion that a Lafite is better than a Larose.

Or so, at least, I have found.

EDWARD HYAMS

CHAPTER ONE

NATURE'S VINEYARD

FRANCE is a natural vineyard: from very remote times the grape-vine has been native there, a fact which we know from fossil remains of species closely related to the vine of history, *Vitis vinifera*. The soil, the geographical situation, the climate of the country, seem to have been designed to produce wine—not, indeed, in the vast quantities which are possible farther south, for example in Algeria and even in Italy, but wines of the finest quality, setting the standard for the whole world. Even the character of the people seems to have been produced for the purpose of making fine wines. For in this art, as in others, the sureness of taste peculiar to the French, the care which they are always ready to give to a task when the object is to make something as well as it can possibly be made, and the instinct for quality rather than mere quantity, are outstanding.

And by a happy coincidence the sort of country and the sort of weather which are essential to the making of fine wines are also what we may, for the purpose of this book, call holiday country and holiday weather. The grape-vine, while it will tolerate winters of great harshness with temperatures as low as −20° F., needs the warm, wet spring weather which creates a green and pleasant land, enough rain in early summer to keep it so, and unbroken fine weather during the late summer and the early autumn to bring the grapes to that perfection which depends upon warmth and sunshine.

Thus a prospective holiday-maker planning his holiday could do much worse than begin by asking himself— where do wine grapes flourish? For where they flourish he will find the sort of country which is pleasing to the eye, even though the very necessities of grape-growing do entail, to be quite honest, a certain amount of damage to the scenery, as we shall see when we get to Burgundy. And he will find the kind of weather which, as a rule, holiday-makers hope for, without ever being sure of.

He will—our imaginary holiday-maker—find a great deal more than that, however, in the great vineyard regions of Europe, but especially of France. For example, and naturally enough, good food and good wine tend to go together. Bordeaux, greatest wine centre in the world, city of the clarets, is famous for its superb cuisine; so too is Lyon, centre of Burgundy. And the Champagne lands of the north-east, the vineyard parishes of the Rhône, the Dordogne, the Moselle, all considerable wine rivers, are all famous for their cooking. And it is a fact that people who eat and drink really well—in the case of the French wine lands better than any other people anywhere in the world—are, at least in public, cheerful, good-natured, fond of laughter, self-indulgent and therefore indulgent to others. From our point of view, then, they are holiday people. Accustomed to the comforts of good wine and the best food, they understand comfort in all its other aspects. They are, in short, people among whom it is easy to relax and take one's ease. Which presumably is what the holiday-maker is looking for.

Although, as we have seen, the grape-vine is native to France, its cultivation for making wine was introduced from abroad. The reason is a matter of history: Western Asia and Eastern Europe were so far in advance of Western Europe in the arts of civilization during the two or three thousand years before Christ when these arts were being developed, that the movement of all such arts was westward; it only began to flow the other way much later. It was therefore inevitable that whichever people, within the habitat of the wild vine, was the most advanced in farming techniques, would be the first to plant and cultivate the vine for wine. The invention of wine itself, however, was almost certainly before the beginnings of viticulture—the cultivation of the vine. Wild grapes were, and for that matter still are, very plentiful in the region between the Caspian and the Black Seas, in parts of Anatolia, and elsewhere within that part of the world, or within easy reach of it, where civilization began. The cultivation of the vine was probably difficult, for climatic reasons, in Mesopotamia, where the earliest city states sprang up, but it was easy in Syria, Palestine and parts of Egypt. We know now that there was some kind of civilized, or at least not altogether primitive, community at Jericho as much as eight thousand years ago.

Thus vine-growing for wine-making, which must have been discovered when wild grapes, bruised in the gathering, had been left in a clay vessel and had fermented, began in the Near East at a time when the people who lived in France were still in the primitive hunting phase of development and a very long way from that level of culture which is required for any kind of farming, let alone the highly skilled art of fruit-growing.

The 'France', from the point of view of all the arts, of this ancient world, was Egypt. And among the techniques which the Egyptians brought to a fine art was that of wine-making. At a time when the people of Britain and France and even Italy were still hunting wild beasts and gathering wild seeds and fruits and roots for their living, the Egyptians already had scores of famous vineyards, each of which was attached to a temple and called by a religious name. They had selected the better vines of their vineyards and propagated mutations, so that they had both white and red grapes, as well as black ones—all wild grapes are black, excepting for rare 'sports'. They knew all about keeping the stronger, heavier wines for many years so that they would mature and come to a perfection impossible in a young wine of this type. Their best wines were sealed in jars with the date of the vintage, such information as whether the wine was sweet, medium or dry, and in addition the name, virtually the signature, of the superintendent of the vintage and the vineyard.

As the Egyptians, like all great peoples, were merchants and exporters, wine was one of their exports. And it was doubtless as a result of this that wine was first tasted by the more backward peoples of the northern shore of the Mediterranean. Meanwhile, however, other advanced peoples, such as the citizens of Tyre and Sidon and other Phoenician communities who had formed colonies in North Africa (one of which became the Carthage of history), were planting vineyards and making wine, and ultimately exporting wine. So that wine began to flow into Europe from more than one source.

As we know from our own experience and in our own time, advancing peoples, growing nations, begin by importing the products of the arts of peace, and end by making them for themselves—when it is possible. We should certainly grow our own tea and coffee in England if it were climatically possible, as it is, for example, for the Americans. And there was no climatic reason against growing wine in Greece. Greece, as the most advanced of the European peoples at the time we are considering, was first to plant vineyards in Europe. First wine reached them from Egypt via Crete, and from what is now Syria via Thrace. Then the vine itself. And within a few centuries Greece, in turn, became the 'France' of the ancient world, while Egypt declined. It is almost as if one of the conditions necessary for the practice of the arts and sciences at a high level is—plenty of good wine.

The Greeks introduced vine-growing and wine-making to their Sicilian and Italian colonies, while the Carthaginians or the Phoenicians were doing the same for Spain. But France did not have to wait for wine until she could get the art of it from Italy. A Greek colony was settled in the south of France, the capital city being Massilia. That city is now Marseilles. And it was there that the vines were first planted and wine first made in France.

It is a fact that the best wines, the wines with the subtlest flavours, the most exquisite aroma or, as the wine experts call it, 'nose', do not come from the places where the vine flourishes most rampantly. In the great heat of Algeria, southern Italy, Andalusia, and even in the considerable heat of the South of France, the vine, provided it be irrigated, grows fast and big and produces immense crops of grapes. But those grapes, instead of confining their sugar production to what is required to produce an adequate quantity of alcohol upon fermentation, make too much sugar. Now the quantity of alcohol in a wine is a function of the quantity of sugar in the grape. If the grape juice, or *must* as it is called technically, contains 20 per cent of sugars, then the resultant wine will contain about 10 per cent of alcohol. The very finest wines do not contain much more than 12 or 13 per cent alcohol. If the grapes contain, therefore, more than 26 per cent of sugar, either the wine will have more than 13 per cent alcohol and tend to be what is called heavy, though it will improve with keeping, or, since the ordinary wine-yeasts which are responsible for turning sugar into alcohol stop working once the medium in which they find themselves contains more than 16 per cent of alcohol (a rule to which there are a few exceptions), the wine will contain a good deal of sugar even when it is finished and will therefore be sweet. The number of sweet wines which are also very good in other respects is very small indeed, and these wines are produced by special techniques, as we shall see when we get to the famous Château d'Yquem. Now the thing which turns the starch in unripe fruit, including grapes, into sugar, is sunshine and sun-heat. So that, for the production of the very best wines, too much sunshine is almost as undesirable as too little.

Moreover, in the great heat of the south, the vines will 'ripen' all the wood they can make, and therefore produce enormous crops of grapes. There is therefore a temptation to plant them in rich valley or plain soils and reap huge harvests. But grapes grown on soils relatively rich in nitrogen are coarse and low in flavour (this is true of all fruits). Farther north the vines grow rampantly enough on rich soils, but do not ripen all the wood they make. For good ripe wood—in much smaller quantity—it is best to plant on stony soils, poor in nitrogen, and to withhold manure. Such 'dwarfed' vines, if skilfully pruned, produce relatively small crops of very high-flavoured grapes. For the vine is a very adaptable plant, and a variety which in, say, Alsace or Kent can be kept no bigger than a currant bush will in, say, Algeria or California cover as much ground as a forest oak and bear literally several tons of grapes—but grapes of inferior quality.

Not that these facts were known when the vineyards of France began to spread north and west. In all probability there were plenty of farmers and gardeners who jeered at the very idea of growing grapes as far north as the Loire, let alone the Rhine, and only the obstinate determination of the local people to have their own wine set the vine migrating northward until, by the end of the fourth century of our era, it was firmly established in Kent, Gloucestershire and even Norfolk.

The establishment of the great French vineyards took place, for the most part, during the long period when Gaul was the most important western province of the Roman Empire, although it is quite certain the beginnings had been made in Narbonne and at the mouth of the Rhône, as well as elsewhere, much earlier, during the Republican period of Roman history when Gaul was an independent Celtic kingdom or loose congeries of kingdoms, rapidly learning the arts of civilization from their southern neighbours even while engaged in fighting them tooth and nail.

The modern name 'France' is derived, as everyone knows, from the Franks, the German people which, as the Roman Empire fell into decrepitude, conquered Gaul, just as another German people, the Anglo-Saxons, conquered the more remote province of Britain. But whereas in Britain not very much of Romano-British culture seems to have been left after the long series of fifth- and sixth-century wars of invasion were over—excepting in the mountains of Wales—in France the Franks, although they conquered the Gauls in war, seem to have been absorbed by them thereafter. Thus we still think of the French as a 'Latin' people, which is an absurdity from the ethnical point of view since the Gauls were Celts, but which makes sense from the cultural point of view since they intermarried for centuries with the Italians, and their culture was, indeed, Latin. And so it remained. The Franks were not the sort of people who could have developed such a fine art as wine-making: they were soldiers and administrators, but very little else. The art of wine-making was therefore already well established from the Mediterranean to the Rhine by the time the conquest was complete. And the Franks respected it as they respected the arts in general, and allowed themselves to be civilized by their defeated enemies.

The finest wines have always been associated with specific places. Ovid made the name of Falernian immortal, and other Roman place-names meant certain attributes in a wine, just as they do with us, and as they may well have done with the Egyptians thousands of years ago. People who have been justly irritated by some of the excesses of wine-snobbishness are apt to sneer at refinements of this kind, and to say that the idea that a wine of certain superlative qualities can be grown only on the south slope of a certain hill in the region of Bordeaux or Burgundy or on the Rhine, is pretentious nonsense. This is a mistake. It is unquestionably true that the quality of good wine is inextricably involved with the nature of soil and site. Nor is there any mystery about the reason for this. The quality of any fruit is dependent on the kind of 'food' the plant receives. Putting it very roughly, if a fruit tree—and a vine is a fruit tree in this context—is grown on a soil very rich in nitrogen, the fruit will be large, loose in texture, lacking in colour and flavour, though it may be quite sweet. Soils poor in nitrogen produce small, highly coloured, richly flavoured fruits, especially where they are rich in phosphorus and potassium. These are the three principal plant nutrients. But there are scores of others which, although required by the trees and vines only in minute quantities ('trace elements'), have an important effect on the health of the plant, and of course on the quantity and quality of the fruit. We understand the broad outlines of this science of plant nutrition, but the effect of 'trace elements', and even of the exact proportions of the three principal nutrients, is so complex that we are only just beginning to understand it. In due course we may be clever enough to relate the quality of a fruit, such as the grape (and therefore of the wine made from it), exactly to the nature of the soil. We may then be able to say not merely that the soil of the Romanée Conti vineyard in Burgundy does unquestionably produce a wine superior in certain attributes to other, neighbouring soils, but exactly why it does so. At the moment we cannot do this. But the fact that we cannot explain it excepting roughly and in principle does not make it any the less true, and it explains why certain parts of France only, and not the whole country, are famous for their vineyards and their wine. Or, rather, it is part of the explanation, the rest being a matter of climate. There is, we repeat, nothing extraordinary or mysterious about this: it is analogous to the English case of cherry-growing. Cherries are best in east Kent simply because cherries prosper best and produce the most flavoursome fruit on at least fifteen feet of brick-earth, and brick-earths that deep are not to be found everywhere, but only in a few parts of England.

In the case of French wine-growing, however, there are refinements on this, just as there are in the case of English apple-growing. The most important of these refinements is the one concerning the close relationship between certain soils and certain varieties of the vine. You can, of course, grow any of the several thousand varieties of the vine in cultivation, in any viticultural region. But wine of a specific quality is the product not only of a certain soil in a certain climatic region, but of one of several (blended) vine varieties. The famous Pinot vines may produce, for example, a very good wine when planted in a given part of the Burgundian vineyard, but a wine inferior to that of a Gamay variety if planted somewhere on the Loire. These compatibilities and incompatibilities between certain wine varieties and certain soils and climates have emerged in time and are known from experience. The explanation of them is much the same as the explanation of the more general phenomenon dealt with above. A variety, to produce its most richly flavoured berries, may need the principal plant nutrients and trace elements in a proportion which is not so perfectly suitable for some other variety. It is as true of plants as of people that one man's meat is another man's poison. It may well be that one day biochemists will be able to say exactly what relationship there is between the particular 'nose' and flavour of a wine, and the metabolism of the plants which produce the grapes used in making that wine. At present they cannot do so, and we have to plant vines, choose varieties, entirely by experience.

This fact makes the vine-grower extremely conservative about vine varieties. He knows, for example, that the Cabernet vines produce, in the right soils and sites, a wine with particular qualities and that the maintenance of those qualities is vital to his business, because it is for those qualities that a high price is paid, year after vintage year, for his wine. He may know perfectly well that the Cabernet vine is not as fruitful as some other variety, so that if he dug up his Cabernets and planted this other, which is known to produce very good wine elsewhere, he would get a larger crop and have more of his wine to sell. But he does not know, and nobody can tell him, that this other variety will produce the same fine qualities in its wine. In fact, experience tends to show that it would not. True, there is probably, among the thousands to choose from, a variety which *would* give him wine of equal quality and in greater quantity. But how to find out, without a very great risk of losing his reputation for wine of a certain quality, since the only way would be to scrap his Cabernets and plant something else 'on spec'? All over the vineyard regions of France are being grown varieties of the vine which bear small crops, relative to what other varieties can do; which are extremely susceptible to spring frosts; which require twelve or fourteen sprayings with copper-lime (Bordeaux mixture) and dusting with sulphur in a single season if they are to be kept free of fungus diseases; which are, in short, both troublesome and expensive to cultivate. And although scores of other varieties which have none of these disadvantages are known, and do well in other parts of the country, yet the old varieties are kept because their performance is known, the quality of their wine established, and that established quality is worth a lot of money to the growers in every vintage year.

This has given rise to a furious controversy which you may well hear echoes of as you make your tour of the vineyards. It may, with reservations, be called the controversy between the exponents of wine-growing as an art, and the exponents of wine-growing as a science. It will be well for you to know a little about it if you are to appreciate the meaning of the raised voices and brandished fists which, as you sit quietly drinking your pint of wine in the corner of a café in the Beaujolais or in Avignon, keep you amused.

When, not quite a hundred years ago, the introduction of native vine species from America brought two grave fungus diseases of the vine, and the terrible aphis *Phylloxera vastatrix*, to Europe, the French vineyards were nearly wiped out. They were saved by sulphur dusting against the oidium, by copper-lime spraying against the mildew, and by grafting the European vines on to American vine roots, resistant to *Phylloxera*. All these devices are both clumsy and very expensive, so that even though the vineyards were saved and wine-making continued, these three American plagues were unquestionably a terrible disaster.

It soon occurred to the more imaginative vine-growers that the thing to do was to breed a new vine, by crossing the best French varieties, with their known quality of fruit and wine, with the American varieties with their resistance to the fungus and aphis troubles which were so deadly to European vines, just because, being foreign to them, the vines possessed no natural resistance to the parasites. During the past sixty years, accordingly, many plant breeders have been at work trying to produce a vine, or many varieties of vine, with a combination of French quality and American robustness. Only in the last ten or fifteen years have the products of these breeding programmes been really good, however. There are now quite a number of man-made varieties which, (*a*) are *almost* as resistant to mildew, oidium and *Phylloxera* as their American parent species, and (*b*) bear *almost* as good grapes, producing very good wine, as their French parent. And what is very important, owing to the phenomenon known to geneticists as 'hybrid vigour', these varieties often (but not always) bear these good grapes in quantities far larger than do the old vines.

Nevertheless, there is, for the reasons already explained, great hostility to the idea of planting them, and indeed it is strictly forbidden to do so within the regions whose wines are in the category of *Appellation Controllée*—literally 'controlled brand-names', under the laws administered by the Comité National des Appellations d'Origine des Vins et

Eaux-de-vie. A wine in this class has to be guaranteed made of certain grapes grown on certain sites and nowhere else; in return, its name is protected; no other wine can claim to be the same or use the same name. Very recently, owing to the fact that the wines made from certain hybrid varieties have consistently won, or received high places, in the great regional and national wine-tastings, a limited number of the new vines has received official approval for planting in the main vineyard areas, but not on the most famous sites, the *côtes* of thin, poor soil which produce the finest wines but in relatively small quantities.

The controversy between the advocates of the new vines, who are for the most part small-holding wine-growers producing good, non-vintage table wine which does not compete with the great named wines, and the staunch conservatives who believe that the French should stick to the proved varieties for all their disadvantages, and that the planting of hybrid new vines should be banned by law, has been and still is extraordinarily bitter. The hybrid-growers believe and say that the secret power-behind-the-throne of the conservative, anti-hybrid party is the parliamentary lobby of the manufacturers of copper and sulphur fungicides, who are said to be afraid that widespread planting of the new disease-resistant varieties will seriously injure their trade. And, of course, it will. Progress, in whatever direction, always hurts somebody. Another argument against growing the hybrid vines was that the French wine-growing industry was, until a year or two ago, apparently suffering from over-production, and to save the small growers the French government was persuaded by the wine-growers' lobby to buy up the surplus and distil it into commercial alcohol which, however, was in excess of demand for that spirit. Since it is claimed that the hybrids produce larger and more regular crops than the old vines, it was argued that their planting would aggravate this unfortunate state of affairs. This argument, however, has been vitiated by the fact that three bad years have turned over-production into a severe shortage of wine. And the hybrid growers can prove that this could not have happened if their vines had been planted in sufficient numbers.

However, the hybrid vines are still excluded from most of those sites with which we are concerned here, the principal wine-growing regions of France. The one which produces the greatest range of great wines, both red and white, will be the right place for us to set foot in France and begin our tour.

We can reach Bordeaux by train via Paris, or by car by driving down the Atlantic side of France from the Channel ports; or the enterprising traveller may even be able to get passage on a ship trading in wine between London river and the mouth of the Gironde. People who do not enjoy real travelling can, of course, fly.

CHAPTER TWO

SAUTERNES, BARSAC AND GRAVES

IT will be as well for any wine-novice setting out to improve his knowledge of wine by spending a holiday in
one or more of the vineyard regions of France, to prepare
not only his palate and his stomach for this pleasant ordeal
but likewise his mind. His first step in this direction should
be to dismiss everything he has ever learnt about wine in
England. True, not quite all of it is arrant nonsense, and a
certain amount of this information will in due course be
rehabilitated. But by that time it will have been properly
tested in the field.

Wine has become the object of one of the most ridiculous
manifestations of snobbery in our snobbish country. The
reason for this is simple: wine has not been grown or made
in Britain as an ordinary commercial activity since roughly
A.D. 1400. In the five and a half centuries since it ceased to
be a sound economic proposition to cultivate the vine in
southern Britain, wine has been imported. And since it is
not a staple of our diet and is in competition with the
immensely rich and powerful brewing interests, no effort
has been made to keep the imports cheap. Even in free-
trading times the price of wine was inflated by Customs
duties. Thus, throughout the centuries when the majority
of British people were relatively poor, with no money for
what is considered a luxury, wine became a high-class drink.

Articles for consumption which are the subjects of a class
distinction, and of showing off by 'conspicuous consumption', always tend to become snob-objects. Oysters, once
the food of the poor in the south-east, have suffered this

change. And if kippers were expensive they would unquestionably undergo the same metamorphosis: they would
become a suitable subject for conversation in well-to-do
circles, would be classified by quality differences, would
have quality differences imagined for them where none
exist, and their value thus inflated by a social phenomenon
having nothing whatever to do with their status as food or
with the laws of supply and demand. They would tend to
go on rising in price as they became, increasingly, the
object of a high-class racket.

To some extent this has been the case with wine. But
this does not mean that the fine distinctions drawn between
the wines of one region and another, one parish and the next,
one vineyard and its neighbour, have no validity. It only
means that talk and writing about wine have a good deal
outrun the realities. For example, there is a commercial
vested interest on the part of wine-merchants, and a social
one on the part of wine-snobs, in maintaining that the order
of merit in which the wines of Bordeaux were arranged for
convenience in 1855, and about which we shall have something to say presently, is an immutable law of nature. For
this reason the common wine-snob will always find a Lafite
or a Haut-Brion superior to a Lascombes or a Pichon-
Longueville, without any regard to the evidence of his
palate; on the other hand, the subtler, more advanced wine-
snob will get a particular satisfaction out of maintaining
that an unknown wine from a forgotten corner of Pauillac
is really better than Château Margaux of a good year: this
is the sort of wine-snob it is good fun to be.

Begin by forgetting this famous order of merit. Then,
when you are in the Bordelais and can taste the wines on the
spot, you can look at the list, printed as Appendix I to this
volume, and decide, if your palate is good enough which is
very doubtful, whether it makes sense. Quite likely the
order of merit in question was valid in 1855. And since the
price received for wine tended to follow the same order,
the owners of the first 'growths', as we call them, the
French word being *crus*, had a powerful economic incentive
to maintain their priority. Their wine has remained magnificent because one way of doing this was to keep the wine

better than others. But the owners of growths which were relegated by the authorities to the second, third, fourth and fifth categories had an equally powerful incentive to improve their wines with a view to getting into the top class, for they were not to know that an order which was established for the benefit of buyers at that time was going to be fixed for ever like the 'laws of the Medes and Persians which alter not'. What maintains the order unchanged is not only the hard reality of superior quality, for no genuine wine expert can dispute that if an impartial reassessment were made today some clarets would be demoted and others promoted; it is real quality plus natural conservatism, plus vested interest plus wine snobbery in the importing countries. The rigidity of the rule is justified by its supporters as follows: they say that certain soils, and *only* those soils, planted with certain varieties of the vine, and *only* those varieties, producing grapes in certain quantities controlled by density of planting and by standardized pruning, must inevitably yield the best wine. So that, for example, the wine from Château Mouton-Rothschild cannot be quite as good as the wine from Château Lafite because Mouton-Rothschild is not on the best site of the Médoc region. But not only is this a questionable argument, it is to some extent invalidated by the fact that 1855, when the classification was made, was before the *Phylloxera* epidemic; that the use of grafting on American rootstocks which that made necessary slightly alters the performance of the fruiting varieties; and that, in any case, there are hundreds, perhaps thousands, of possible combinations of good varieties of the vine with a given soil which have yet to be tried.

The first thing to get out of your mind, then, is prejudice about quality based on names only. But do not be too radical about it, for it is absolutely true that certain wine names do mean very high quality in a wine; and that, although the order of merit needs overhauling, it is for the most part still roughly viable.

Another thing to forget is a good deal of what you know about wine-glasses. A burgundy glass should be large and not more than half-filled; a claret glass is, conventionally, smaller, and often filled right up. Drink claret out of a bur-

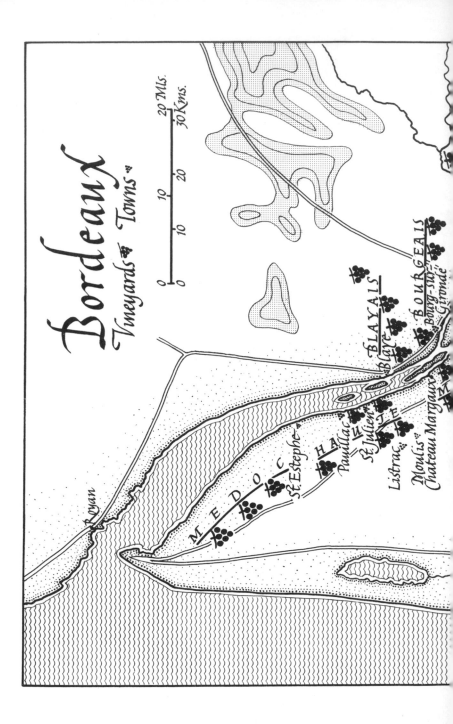

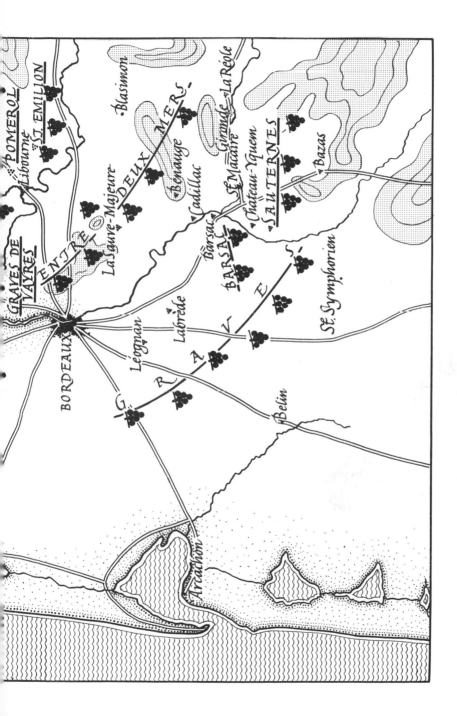

gundy glass and only half-fill the glass. Never drink champagne out of a champagne glass, it is the wrong shape for sparkling wines. Champagne should be drunk from a tall, narrow glass which retains the sparkle. Never drink brandy from a balloon glass, it is silly and pretentious: drink it from a whisky glass.

If, however, you know any wine-jargon, it would be a pity to forget that. Even if most of it is twaddle, it is amusing to use and to listen to, and does no more harm than quoting poetry. In any case, we have only the crudest terms for the sensations experienced by the palate, and this fact alone justifies at least some of the whimsicalities in which people indulge when talking or writing about wine. Wine jargon, such as the comparing of a wine to velvet and violets, is all right, provided you do not take it too seriously.

It might be objected that the whole subject is being taken too seriously here, that the author is being didactic about something which should be shrugged off as trivial. But this is not so. Wine is important. It is important not only because it is one of life's few absolutely reliable pleasures, and if not abused a source of health, but because the sensations it affords are worth cultivating in the same way as the other pleasures of the senses. The ear has to be taught to appreciate music, to distinguish the good from the bad and enjoy the greater pleasure afforded by the good. The eye has to be educated to pick out good painting from bad painting, and the education is worth undertaking because the pleasure to be afforded by good painting, not to mention the instruction, is so very much greater than that yielded by bad painting. The palate, too, has to be taught to yield a higher pleasure from exquisite sensations than from coarsely agreeable ones, and the most exquisite sensations of which the palate is capable are afforded by fine wines and the best apples; they are to the sense of taste what the works of the great composers are to the sense of hearing.

The best state of mind in which to approach a wine holiday, even if you know something about wine, is that of the uninformed man willing to learn.

*   *   *   *   *   *

The three greatest wine rivers in the world, with all due respect to the Sâone, are the Garonne, the Dordogne and the Isle, all of which become the Gironde at Bordeaux. And by a fortunate coincidence the country through which they flow is very lovely in its variety, its diverse charms, its range. It includes mountains, with the dramatic and exciting gorges of the Tarn which is a tributary of the Garonne; rich agricultural land worked with everything from the latest tractors to teams of oxen; soft and gentle hills; glorious forests; pine-lands and sandy flats and delightfully desolate sea-coast. Above all there are the rivers themselves, sometimes slow and deep and stately, at others rushing turbulent, over shallow and rocky beds, or tumbling noisily through narrow gorges and over rapids. The land of the Dordogne is particularly beautiful and attractive to visitors. For those who are interested in the past of our race there are the caves of Lascaux where, about twenty thousand years ago, some of the earliest men of the true *Homo sapiens* species painted the walls of their dwellings, or perhaps cave-temples, with marvellously executed paintings of the great beasts they hunted for a living, thus proving that even so long ago this strange and beautiful country of river plains and inland cliffs was already populated by men of artistic genius and developed taste. For those who are amateur, or even professional, botanists, the high country of the Tarn is fragrant with narcissus and a thousand other flowers in May, and in the neighbourhood of Lascaux the most spectacular of the European wild orchids, the Lizard Orchid, which is such a rarity in England, can be seen in thousands.

A tour of the French vineyards is a tour of the French rivers. It is circular, and as the place where you begin to go round a circle is both your beginning and end, I shall start in the Roussillon but leave its wines until last. One of the principal sources of the Garonne rises in the Roussillon, on the French side of the Pyrenees; another in the Jurançon, farther west in the same range. These two streams join at Toulouse and thence flow, as the Garonne, between the countries of Gaillac on the right bank and Armagnac on the left.

Armagnac grows grapes but not for wine, or rather the

wine they yield is not the 'end-product', since it is distilled into brandy, the only brandy in the world which can compete with Cognac. The growers of this region are smallholders, but the distillation is carried out by co-operatives or firms which, although large, are not as large as those of Cognac. Consequently the brandies of Armagnac are more diverse than those of Cognac, and by that much more interesting. Nor are the brandies the only interesting thing in Armagnac. Its towns of stone, ancient, crenellated, arcaded, are attractive, and the city of Auch has a splendid specimen for collectors of bad architecture, the sixteenth-century cathedral: and for musicians, the unmodified seventeenth-century organ in that cathedral.

More nonsense is talked about brandy than even about wine. First, on the subject of age: it is very doubtful whether brandy goes on improving for ever. It probably needs from twenty-five to thirty years to reach perfection, but certainly not a hundred years. The kind of Cognac which has the colour of boot-polish and the texture of sump-oil should be avoided; by avoiding it, especially if its label claims some Methuselah-like age for it, good money can be saved and nothing lost, since really fine Cognac is thin, and pale gold in colour like illicitly distilled whisky. The darker colour of pretentious brandies is apt to be due to burnt sugar. Brandy from Armagnac, however, is naturally darker than brandy from Cognac. But it should not be oily and there is no point whatsoever in paying extra for spirit which is more than a quarter of a century old. I have sometimes wondered whether the brandy-distillers' obsession with age is due to the fact that, by comparison with their neighbours the vintners, their product is a *parvenu*. Wine is as old as civilization, or rather older. But brandy, the product of distilled wine, is barely a thousand years old. Distillation was invented by Arab chemists, and it can hardly have been introduced to Europe before about the twelfth century. And this mania for very old brandy has led to some unfortunate practices, not only the spoiling of colour and texture with burnt sugar, but worse, or at least even less honest. Heaven forbid that I should think ill of any man in the trade of wines and spirits, but it is said that when an unquestionably ancient bottle or two of brandy come on to the market from the private cellar of a deceased gentleman, the blenders will buy it, pour it into a thousand times its bulk in sound, youngish brandy and sell the lot as a hundred years old. Some such practice is indeed necessary to explain the continued existence in our midst of 'Napoleon' brandies, unless we are to suppose that in the time of that emperor all the great rivers of France flowed with the stuff.

The distillers of Armagnac are not under such severe commercial strains as their competitors of Cognac, for their brandies have become known and popular only quite recently, as these things are reckoned. And it is quite possible that their claim to produce better brandies than do the men of Cognac may now have become true.

However, Armagnac is not wine country. I know little about brandy, and I shall spend no more time on it. Still following the Garonne and still well to the south-east of Bordeaux, at a point where the river takes a turn due west, on its south-west bank is the region of Sauternes. This is the first famous wine region we come to moving downstream.

Sauternes and Barsac, lying south of the Graves, is a region of intensive viticulture consisting of five *communes*, which can be roughly, incorrectly, but expediently translated as 'parishes'. Nearly all the wine made in this region is white and more or less sweet. As throughout the whole of the Bordelais, the most famous vineyards are centred upon châteaux. Not only are the grapes grown on the château estate, but all the processes of wine-making from pressing to bottling are carried out there. Not all the wine of the châteaux is bottled at the châteaux, but only the best. The rest, varying from good to . . . well, less good, is sold in bulk to shippers for bottling.

This is the point at which to consider the validity of the order of merit referred to above, and to glance for the first time at the grading of wines by quality, a subject to which we can give more attention when we come to the Médoc, farther north.

Under the law of *Appellation Controllée* the growers and makers of certain wines have rights and obligations. Their principal right is protection against the use of their wine's name by any other grower or vintner. Their obligations, as already mentioned, are to plant only certain of their soils, to plant only certain varieties of the vine, to prune and cultivate them in the manner laid down, and to avoid certain practices which may, however, be perfectly legal elsewhere. The rights and obligations under this law are conferred, and laid upon, only such wines as conform to a given high standard.

Within the Sauternes and Barsac region there are vineyards attached to châteaux, and others which are not, but the latter may also have the right to the name Sauternes, or Barsac, on their wine labels. These names are, as explained, therefore *place*-names which, when they appear on a wine label, have a definite significance. An Australian or American, South African or Spanish grower who puts the word 'Sauternes' on his labels is suggesting that his wines have, in fact, come from France, and I think wines so labelled should be avoided. The good wines of the four countries mentioned are labelled with their own place-names, and not with those of the French vineyards.

I shall leave the explanation of the classification of wines in order of merit by place until we come to the Médoc, but it is equally valid and important in the Sauternes, and the full list is printed in Appendix I. And the rule for judgement free of prejudice which I have dared to suggest in the section on the Médoc wines, is just as applicable to the Sauternes and the Barsac wines.

The shipper who bottles wine bought in bulk from a château has the right to label it with the name of that château, and if your wine-merchant and his shipper are both honest men—and there are as many honest men in the wine trade as out of it and probably rather more—when you buy a wine with such a label on the bottle you will be buying a fine wine. But not the finest; nor, of course, paying the highest price. The best wines produced at a château vineyard are not sold in bulk but bottled on the premises, and the château label on a bottle of such wine will have a rubric stamped across it: *Mise en bouteille au château*, that is, 'bottled at the château'.

Sauternes contains what is perhaps the most famous wine-château on earth, the only one which is known to hundreds of thousands of people by name, though they have never tasted the wine and perhaps never tasted *any* château-bottled wine in their lives. Several thousand people have heard of Château d'Yquem for every one who has ever tasted it (if only because it is very expensive!).

The château itself is a handsome building in conventional château style, built in the late sixteenth century on the site and within the bastions of a twelfth-century castle. Its regular and exquisitely neat vineyards—not a weed to be seen!—come right down to the foot of its walls in places, but there is also a well-kept garden of fine lawns and rose-beds, and some impressive 'clumps' of trees rather in the English taste.

There is a peculiarity in the technique of making the best sweet Sauternes wines, one which entails making a blessing of what in other vineyards is regarded as a curse. The grapes at Château d'Yquem, Château Filhot, Château Suduiraut and some others are, like grapes everywhere, attacked by the fungus parasite *Botrytis cinerea*—the same *Grey Mould* which often sends up the price of strawberries in England by destroying half the crop. But the sweet Sauternes are made from grapes which have been attacked by this fungus. The harvest is gathered not by clearing the crop at one picking, but by picking over the grapes several times, the pickers using scissors and taking only those parts of the bunches which are, as it were, rotten-ripe. This is one of the reasons for the very high prices charged for these wines.

The advantage conferred by the *Botrytis* fungus is as follows: by drawing water from the grapes it leaves the sugar content relatively higher than it would otherwise have been even in the case of fully ripe grapes. So that when the wine is made, not only is it very high in alcohol, but some sugar remains. Hence, in the *communes* of Sauternes and Barsac *Botrytis cinerea* is honoured with the title *Pourriture noble*—the noble rot.

Visitors interested in seeing for themselves how grapes are grown, stripped from the stalks, pressed, fermented, matured and bottled—in short, visiting a château—can arrange it by addressing their request to the nearest *Syndicat d'Initiative.* Every considerable town has one, and one of its functions is public relations. At Château d'Yquem the visitor will see wine-making apparatus which is unique in the world, for even its working parts, or such of them as may be in contact with the *must* or the wine, are made of wood.

Still keeping to the Garonne, but not yet moving farther towards the mouth, we cross the river into the *Entre-deux-mers* country. The 'two seas' in question are not, of course, seas, but the rivers Garonne and Dordogne, and the name is given to all the wines which are made there and which come under the rules of *Appellation Controllée.*

Until five years ago *Entre-deux-mers* wines were, like the wines from across the Garonne, sweet white wines. But a revulsion of the markets away from full-bodied, highly alcoholic, sweet white wines, and in favour of the lighter, dryer whites of Burgundy and Alsace, led the *Entre-deux-mers* growers, less deeply committed by tradition and reputation to the specific qualities associated with Sauternes and Barsac, to change their whole policy and start making dry wines. There can as yet be no opinion as to their quality, but visitors who can try some of them in the region will be able to bring us back the news concerning them.

Entre-deux-mers vineyards, like those of Sauternes and Barsac, are centred on châteaux, the outstanding example being Cadillac, property of the ancient d'Epernon family; or round the establishment of a co-operative grouping numerous small-holders, small-holding being the rule in nearly all the best vineyard regions. (The wine produced from vast vineyards run on industrial lines is always inferior.) Cadillac is well worth a visit quite apart from its wines: it is one of the finest great houses in France, its elaborate baroque fireplaces are world-famous among connoisseurs of such things, and among other attractions it has a 'whispering gallery' room, of extraordinary and amusing acoustic properties. Visitors are charged less than the half-crown fee usual for similar visits to the stately homes of England.

On the south-west bank of the Garonne, across the river from Entre-deux-mers again, is a vineyard region whose name is even more widely known in the world than that of either of its neighbours: Graves. And the same triangle of country, bounded on the west by the Bay of Biscay and on the east by the Garonne, is good holiday country. Arcachon, on its great basin of shallow water, an almost land-locked inlet of the sea, is a famous holiday resort where the French themselves, rather than foreign tourists, go. All the same, I once had a shocking experience there: I was offered English bottled sauces in what had seemed to be a decent restaurant. The French have learnt better since those days and perhaps would not be guilty of such an outrage now. The basin of Arcachon is connected by a waterway with the strange Etang de Lacanau farther north; this *étang*, a mere beside the sea, is haunted by waterfowl. The coastal country is not everybody's taste, it is all sand and pines, and some call it desolate. Certainly, like all estuary landscape, it is melancholy, but there are many people for whom that kind of country has a special charm. Inland, the land rises a little, then falls away, still pine-clad, in gentle slopes towards the estuary: and there is the Graves country, with pines and vines marching together on its westerly fringe. South lies Sauternes, north the Médoc; and the city of Bordeaux itself.

Indeed, the city, and the vineyards of Graves, interpenetrate, so that two of the greatest Graves wines, Haut-Brion, a red of such quality that it was and is included as a First Growth in the order of merit, the others so classified being all Médocs; and La Mission Haut-Brion, are grown and made in what are now virtually suburbs of Bordeaux, with public-transport vehicles, lorries and an endless stream of private cars thundering down the great main road between them.

Most people think of Graves as white wines, but as we have seen, the greatest of them is a red. However, most of the 43 *communes* of the region do produce mainly whites, although there are some other reds. Incidentally, although all red wine has to be made with a majority of black grapes white wine is not necessarily made from white grapes—

in fact many of the most famous, including some champagnes, are made from black grapes. The difference in wine colour is due not (with a few exceptions) to the juice of the grapes but to vinification techniques. The juice of both black and white grapes is, with the exceptions referred to above, more or less colourless. White wine is made by extracting the juice and fermenting it. No fermentation occurs until the liquid is free of the skins, pips and other solids. But red wine is made by crushing black grapes and allowing juice, pulp, skins and pips to ferment together until sufficient colouring matter has been extracted from the skins into the *must*. Only then is the material put through the wine-press, so that what comes out is a red, fermenting *must*. The solids, collectively known as *marc*, are constantly forced to the top of the fermenting vats during the first stage, since they float on the *must*, and also because they are lifted by the action of carbonic acid gas, a by-product of fermentation. The *marc* forms a thick cap, but this is several times a day forced back into the *must* with poles and stirred about, so that the colouring pigment in the skins becomes available to the *must*.

The exceptions among grape varieties are those with coloured juice, and they are known as *teinturier*, literally *dyer*, grapes, and valued in some kinds of wine-making for their rich supply of pigment. Not all black grapes provide a good colour in wine, and there is a tale that some vintners used to use elderberries to dye their wine. As a matter of fact there would be no harm in this; the elderberry makes an excellent wine by itself. But it would certainly not be allowed in the vineyards under the *Appellation Controllée* law. *Teinturier* grapes in sufficient quantity might be used, however, in certain regions.

The red Graves wines all come from grapes of the Merlot, Cabernet, Malbec and Petit Verdot varieties. None of these wines is from a single variety, all contain blends of grapes, each kind of grape imparting to the wine some quality supposedly peculiar to it. It is possible, given the same thin, gravelly soil, to produce wines of similar, though not identical, quality, or at least character, from other kinds of grapes; even—but do not quote this within earshot of

Graves unless you want to be deported as an undesirable alien—from one or two of the best hybrid kinds. I have drunk such wines. But the rules under the *Appellation Controllée* laws are very strict and the growers and vintners of red Graves must stick to the varieties laid down for them.

The *cépages* (i.e. vine varieties), which provide the grapes for the white Graves are Semillon, Sauvignon and Muscadelle. Those authorities who are certain that the strictness of the rules concerning varieties is right, and that no other blend of grapes would produce so fine a wine, forget that these *cépages* replaced other, earlier ones, and that it might just as well be possible to improve on the wines as to spoil them. But this does not mean that the kinds of grapes used to make a given wine are not important. You cannot make good wine with just any old grapes grown in any old soil. There is nothing chi-chi about this: as you will know if you have ever visited the cider country of Somerset and Herefordshire, precisely the same thing is true of apples and cider.

Unlike the Sauternes, white Graves may be either sweet, or medium-dry, or dry.

The Graves château best worth visiting from an architectural point of view, although a number of them are very pleasant places, is in the suburbs of Bordeaux, La Mission Haut-Brion, far more beautiful and more impressive than its opposite number, which perhaps consoles the owners for the superior status of the other château's wine. Both Haut-Brion and La Mission Haut-Brion produce a little white wine, but mostly the famous reds.

La Mission Haut-Brion is a relatively small château, but exquisitely proportioned, so that it compares favourably with any of the more famous great houses of the 'Château country' farther north. What is more, it has an English garden, so much more beautiful than the French kind: for ornamental gardening is an art which, notwithstanding the work of the great pioneer landscapist Le Notre, the French have never really mastered.

Another of the Graves châteaux, La Brède, is a place of literary, as well as oenological, pilgrimage, for it was the home of the philosopher Montesquieu, whose *Esprit des*

Lois has been a standard work for students and professors of social and political philosophy almost since it was published, and despite the fact that it is in part based on the great thinker's total misunderstanding of the English system of Parliamentary democracy, for which he had an exaggerated reverence. La Brède is open to visitors, is surrounded by a moat which teems with pike, and beyond that by fine woods and, of course, vineyards. Very tranquil after the urban uproar of Haut-Brion.

CHAPTER THREE

MÉDOC

APART from the vineyards of the Mediterranean littoral, those of Bordeaux are the oldest established in France. It is virtually certain that the region was well-known, if not famous, for its wines before the end of the first century of our era which, as we shall see, is not the case in any other of the great vineyard regions, unless as is possible, a brilliant beginning had been made in Burgundy, around the ancient city of Vienne.

The successful establishment of vineyards on the rivers Gironde and Rhône was a source of serious loss to the great wine-growers of Italy. Rivers were, at that period, by far the most important means of inland freight-carrying, and the rivers of Gaul had been used by Italian wine-shippers, as described by Diodorus Siculus, to send their goods to the northern limits of the Roman Empire and even farther. But once it was clear that wine could successfully be grown halfway or more than half-way along the trade routes between the Italian vineyards and their most distant markets, it became obvious that the days of enormous profits for the Italian vintners were over. Trimalchio, Petronius' ridiculous *nouveau riche*, boasting at dinner of how he had cheerfully borne the loss of five wine-laden ships years ago, adds 'Yet wine, at the time, was worth its weight in gold'.[1] The implication clearly is that this price had since fallen sharply, and Professor Roger Dion's researches have revealed that this was, in fact, the case. Italian wine-merchants were having to face severe competition from the Gironde, and possibly from southern Burgundy.

The Italians were quite right to be worried; they could

[1] *The Satiricon: '. . . tunc erat contra aurum'.*

not know, but they could foresee, that the time would soon come, as it did, when the direction of wine commerce would be reversed and wine would begin to flow not out of Italy into Gaul, but out of Gaul into Italy. True, for generations, Falernian was to remain the greatest of wines (references to it are to be found not only in Ausonius and Sidonius Apollinaris, but as late as Gregory of Tours). But for good-quality wines, for ordinary day-to-day drinking, Gaul threatened to oust Campania.

It was this danger which drove the Italian wine-merchants to bring pressure to bear on the government to put a stop to provincial competition. The historian Suetonius says: 'Convinced that the superabundance of wine and the short-age of wheat were due to an excessive craze for planting vineyards, such that ordinary agriculture was being neg-lected, the Emperor [Domitian] prohibited new planting in Italy and ordered the grubbing up of at least half the vine-yards in the provinces.'

It is a fact that Domitian's decree was not successful, if that was its intention, in putting a stop to French viti-culture: in fact Suetonius says he gave up trying to enforce it. Still, there was official hostility to the trade and this would have been sufficient to prevent the northerly extension of the vineyards until, in A.D. 280, the edict was reversed by another emperor, Probus. Consequently, the vineyards of Bordeaux and possibly those about Vienne in Burgundy are at least a couple of centuries older than the other French vineyards of the north, and much more than two centuries older than the most recent and most northerly of all, Champagne.

*   *   *   *   *   *

North-west of Bordeaux those rivers which, up to Bor-deaux, were the Garonne, Dorgogne, Isle and Tarn become the Gironde, a long, wide estuary which connects Bordeaux with the sea and makes it the greatest wine-port in the world. It has held this position for many centuries. Its clarets are called, after the estuary, 'wines of the Gironde'.

Still keeping west of the river, between it and the coast

towards the tip of the great vineyard triangle, the first important wine region we come to is the Haut Médoc, north of which lies the Médoc, the mouth of the Gironde, and the sea. The coast here, again, with the two meres of Lascanau and Carcans, has the melancholy charm of estuary country with its great flat spaces, its pines, its confusion of land and water, and its wildfowl. Inland, however, towards the estuary coast, the whole land is one of vineyards. And for many wine lovers the two Médocs produce the greatest wines in the world, towering above even the great Burgundies in stature. This, however, is prejudice. There is a great deal of point in comparing one red Bordeaux wine with another, even a Médoc with a St. Emilion if you like. But there is no point at all in comparing the wines of one region with those of another and remote region where soil, climate, *cépages* and techniques of vinification are different. There are occasions for listening to Beethoven, and others for listening to Bach, and you may prefer one composer to another. But you cannot say that one is "greater" than the other. So with wines; the wine of Médoc is of one kind, that of Burgundy of another. There are occasions for claret, and occasions for burgundy, often at the same meal. They should not be regarded as competing, but as completing each other.

Moreover, Médoc wines, and Burgundy wines, are made in different conditions. Leaving aside the highly technical matter of soil differences, the climatic difference is relatively great. For any part of the Bordeaux region, especially the Médoc, to go so short of sun throughout a whole summer and autumn as to leave the grapes with too little sugar to make the requisite body of the wine, is extremely rare. The problem is more likely (although this too is rare, in the Médoc) to be one of sugar residue after fermentation. In Sauternes it is that residue which makes the wines sweet. In Burgundy the case is quite different. In the first place Lyon, south of the Burgundy vineyards, is nearly a hundred miles farther north than Bordeaux. Moreover, whereas the Bordeaux wine region is under the mild influence of the Atlantic, like our own Cornwall, Burgundy is under the climatic influence of the high Alps. In many years the grapes in many parts of the Burgundy vineyards end the season short of sugar, and *chaptelisation*, the addition of cane sugar to the *must*, is practised, under certain rules of the laws governing wine-making, in order that the wine shall have a sufficient degree of alcoholic strength. As we shall see, this is also the case in Alsace and in Champagne.

We have said that the Médoc is by some considered the world's greatest vineyard. In justification, its *communes* include Margaux, St. Julien, St. Estephe, Pauillac. Châteaux, every one bearing a name which one has read in good wine-lists all one's adult life, are thick on that sandy, gravelly ground which was formerly the bottom of a shallow sea.

The famous order of merit of Bordeaux wines has been referred to already: it was made, as we have said, in 1855, and only four wines were put into the class of First Growths. Of these, three are Médocs, the fourth being a Graves, Haut-Brion. The three Médocs are:

Château Lafite, in Pauillac
Château Latour, in Pauillac
Château Margaux, in Margaux

Margaux also has four second growths:

Château Rausan-Segla
Château Rausan-Gassies
Château Dufort-Vivien
Château Lascombes

The three Pauillac second growths are:

Château Mouton-Rothschild
Château Pichon-Longueville (Baron de Pichon)
Château Pichon-Longueville (Comtesse de Lalande)

The *commune* of St. Julien has no first growth but five seconds:

Château Léoville-Las-Cases
Château Léoville-Poyferré
Château Léoville Barton
Château Gruaud-Larose
Château Ducru-Beaucaillou

The *commune* of St. Estephe has two second growths:

Château Cos d'Estournel
Château Montrose

For the rest, the list is printed in full under Appendix I. Roughly speaking, there are three kinds of Médoc which you can drink, according to your means and taste. Beginning at the bottom, you can drink a bottle of wine which is simply labelled *Médoc*. It will contain wine from one of the lesser vineyards of the region; or wine which has been bought in bulk from various châteaux and is not good enough to receive the château label. In a bad year there may be a lot of this. Nevertheless, even a nameless Médoc should be a sound and honest wine.

Going a step up the scale, you can buy a bottle labelled *St. Julien, Margaux, Pauillac,* that is to say, with the name of a Médoc *commune.* The wine in the bottle will not come from just anywhere within the Médoc, but from one *commune,* and again it will be from a nameless vineyard or it will be wine from a great vineyard which is just not quite up to the standard which the châteaux have to set themselves if they do not want to lose their reputation. Such wine will be a little better, a little more distinguished, and a little dearer than plain Médoc.

Next up the scale will be a bottle labelled Château So-and-So. This bottle will contain wine grown at the château in question, say Margaux or Lascombes, bought in bulk by a shipper in Bordeaux, bottled by him either in Bordeaux or in, for example, London. The label will therefore bear not only the château name, but also the shipper's name, which is important since although it is well known that all wine-shippers are honest men, some are more honest than others and would not dream of putting Algerian wine, however good—and much of it is excellent—into a bottle claiming to contain the wine of a named château.

Finally, the top of the scale: this is a bottle labelled Château So-and-So and cross-stamped *Mise en bouteille au château.* Such a wine will cost a lot of money and it should be well worth what it costs provided you have a palate for wine, of which more anon.

It would, however, be altogether too convenient if that were all. But it would also be a very singular dispensation of Providence if every château in the Médoc and elsewhere in the Bordelais happened to be on a superior site and soil for wine-growing. In fact, of course, this is not the case: all the châteaux capable of producing *grands crus* wines are in the 1855 list. But there are other châteaux, not in the list but putting their names on their labels. Their wines may be what are called *crus bourgeois*, or even *crus artisans*, and not 'royal' or 'noble' wines at all. A château wine is not, therefore, invariably one of the fine wines; the château in question must be 'on the list'.

There are people who complain that from £1 to as much as £4 is an outrageous price to pay for a bottle of wine, and that no wine can be worth it. Let them drink beer, or even Coca-Cola if they like. It has taken several centuries of what is hideously called 'know-how', the care of a soil which can very easily be unbalanced by a mistake in manuring or cultivation, the tending of thousands of plants which are subject to very serious diseases and are difficult to please; the application of five or six sulphur dustings and up to twelve copper sprayings every year to every vine; winter and summer pruning by very highly skilled workers; the capitalization of much expensive machinery; the annual purchase by each château of something like ten thousand pounds' worth of new oak barrels, not to mention bottles and corks which are also very expensive; the making of the wine, and then keeping it for four or five years at least, which again has to be capitalized. Moreover, it has entailed the rejection of part of the crop, part of the wine, as imperfect; and sometimes, in bad years, of the whole crop. 'Little' wines can be made quite cheaply and very nice they are, too; I drink some every day of my life. But the making of great wines is an extremely expensive business and whoever wants to enjoy the keenest pleasure the palate can confer, has to pay for it.

It will be realized that the classification of Bordeaux wines by merit is very complicated. Not only is there the order of châteaux, there is the order of wines within a given *commune*. Will a château-bottled wine from a fifth-growth château, say Château Pontet-Canet in Pauillac, be better than, or not so good as, an unidentified Margaux, or a Château Margaux bottled by a shipper? As a rule, the answer is 'certainly' in the first case and 'probably', in the second. But there are some other factors to consider.

First of all, the common wine-drinker, that is ourselves, simply cannot make these finer distinctions. Certainly, if we have any palate at all, we shall be able to taste the difference between any château *grand cru* wine *mise en bouteille au château*, and an unidentified Médoc, or even an otherwise unidentified Margaux or Pauillac. And a wine palate, by the way, is cultivated, not born. But I do not believe that the ordinary wine-drinker can taste the difference or attribute superior merit, as between, say, a first- and fifth-growth château-bottled wine. No test is fair unless it is made blind: if a man be given a first-growth wine, say a Lafite of a good year, and a fifth, say a Mouton d'Armailhacq of the same year, and is told in advance what he is drinking, he will find for the Lafite because he is unconsciously influenced by the order of merit as by law established. But let the same man be given the same wines blind, and he will as often as not either find no difference, or he will place the fifth-growth wine before the first.

Do not fall into the error of thinking that this is because the ordinary wine-drinker is a sensible chap and that the distinctions made by more experienced wine-drinkers are all pretentious clap-trap. A few men—a very, very few—can, by tasting, place a wine in its vineyard and year. The distinctions are there all right, but it takes years of daily and discriminating wine-drinking to detect them. When you can do it, a source of new and refined pleasure is open to you. But there is this to be said, or rather repeated: that although the order of merit is still roughly valid, it is certainly not valid in detail and all the time, and it is perfectly possible for a fourth- or fifth-growth wine really to be better than a first. And there are some second- and third-growth wines which are consistently as good as firsts, for example Lascombes, and Cos d'Estournel.

This is worth knowing, and it is worth while for the visitor to the Médoc to try and find out what the knowing locals consider the best fourth- and fifth-growth wines, because the common wine-drinker can get a lot of pleasure and save a good deal of money in the course of educating his palate to understand the great Médocs. If, on some subsequent occasion, your company is knowing about wine, or thinks it is, there is a lot of fun to be had out of saying, as you look up from the wine list: 'I want you to try the Mouton d'Armailhacq of thirty-five. It is, as of course you know, a fifth-growth wine, but in my view it is more interesting than the Lafite of the same year.' There will always be one man in your company who thinks that this is a gambit for saving money; such people are best ignored. There will be a woman who thinks you are bluffing. She will continue to think so whatever you say. There may be someone who really knows about wine; if he is civil he will agree with you; if he is over-earnest, his reasons for disagreeing will be stated courteously, and with regard to your own, different, opinion, and will make quite good conversation. Most of your guests will, if you state your opinion with a sufficient air of authority, believe you. But—and here is the point—do not bluff. You will probably get away with it, but that is not the point. The game is only amusing if you really do think, albeit knowing that you may be wrong, that the fifth-growth wine you have chosen is better than the first of its year.

About the dates of wine, the 'vintages' of Médoc. Very good years of two different kinds occur: there are years, generally heat-wave years, which produce wine which will be outstandingly good after a long, sometimes a very long, time in which to mature: these are the very full-bodied wines, the wines described as *corsé*. It is no good drinking them young, for they will not be ready. There are also good years which produce wines which achieve their balance, their maturity, more quickly. Conditions of wind and rain, sunshine and cloud, differ every year, there is no such thing as an 'average' year excepting in the imagination of meteorological statisticians. You cannot buy a really bad wine under a *grand cru* château-bottled label, because the wine of the bad years is never so bottled, but sold in bulk. But if you are to get the most out of your wine-drinking it is necessary to know which years are likely to be ready for drinking now, and which not. It is no good assuming, as will be clear from the above, that an older wine is necessarily better than a younger one; it simply does not work like that. Wines are alive: they are 'born', they grow up, they mature, age, decline, die. And the age at which they are mature is a function of the weather in the year they were 'born', although unfortunately even the greatest experts can only say very roughly, from a knowledge of that weather, how long a wine is likely to need in bottle before it can be served. The judgement is made by annual tasting of a vintage, after a certain number of years—the wine's years of infancy—have elapsed.

Red Bordeaux have to be older than red Burgundies because they have more body, in any but a freakish year. It would be interesting if some wine-drinking meteorologist with time on his hands would compare, over as long a course of years as possible, the quality of Bordeaux vintages with the behaviour of the weather-system called the *Azores anticyclone*. And a sort of holiday-guide might be compiled for sun-worshippers by reference to the number of years in which a given district produces *corsé* wines. Some Médocs take an astonishing time to grow up: I have never tasted it, and do not even know if it is true, but I have heard it said that the Lafite of 1875 was not really perfect until the nineteen-twenties. This, however, is unusual. Contrary to a popular illusion, wines do not go on improving indefinitely.

It should be clear from the above that a red Bordeaux of, say 1926, is not necessarily more mature than one of 1935, for all it is nine years older. Those dates were chosen deliberately: for it happens that whereas the best Médocs[1] of 1935 are already past their prime, and will now be declining, not improving, those of 1926 have not yet reached their prime and will go on improving for some years.

The following is a short and rough guide to the château Médocs of the last forty-odd years in terms of vintages. The

---

[1] When, in this context, I refer to Médocs, I mean château, and even château-bottled, *grand cru* wines. The vintage year of nameless Médocs is not so important, although, since the vines of obscure vineyards are under the same climatic influence, it should not, when it can be known, be ignored.

limit of forty years is suggested by the fact that older wines are no longer to be found on wine-lists—with some rare, and horribly expensive, exceptions.

1921. A heat-wave summer. Very full-bodied wine. Ready to drink, of course, but will go on improving still.

1922. A light and subtle wine. Much has passed its prime and it should be drunk without delay.

1923. Described as 'a supple and well-balanced wine'. Not as light as the 1922, but it will not improve with keeping longer, and some will have passed its best.

1924. A great year. Still far from declining.

1925. Must be drunk at once.

1926. A very full-bodied year. Ready to drink, but improving.

1927. None.

1928. Full-bodied. Not really at its potential best yet.

1929. A great year: still improving.

1930–32. None fit to drink; three very bad years.

1933. Too light. Past their zenith.

1934. A fine, stout year. The wines are not perfect yet.

1935. A light year. Past their zenith and were never very good anyway.

1936. As for 1935.

1937. Very full-bodied. Is barely ready to drink.

1938. An admirably well-balanced year. The wine can be drunk now and will also go on improving for some time.

1939. Will not keep any longer.

1940. A good year. The wine is probably as good as it is ever likely to be.

1941. As for 1939.

1942–1943. Perfectly balanced vintages. The wines are already excellent, but they will still improve.

1944. A light year. The wines will not last very long, but are not in danger of senility yet.

1945. An exceptional year in that although rather full-bodied the wines are already admirable drinking.

1946. Another light vintage, but the wine will gain quality for a year or two.

1947. Full-bodied year. The wines should be kept longer.

1948. As above, not yet at their best.

1949. Lighter than the two previous years and so maturing faster. Young, but can be drunk now.

1950.   Will be very good in some years' time, but they are not ready yet.

1951.   Light, but not ready yet.

1952.   Very well-balanced year. The wine is maturing faster than the 1950, but it is not yet ready.

1953–1957.   None yet fit to drink.

Some of the 1953 wines are being drunk already, but in my view this is a pity. The fact is that it is always possible to drink Médoc wines after, say, five years: but it is not desirable. In the past even the wines of moderate years, the lighter years, would have been kept much longer than they are now, and the reason for drinking them younger now has nothing to do with a discovery that they do not need as much maturing as used to be thought: it is simply that there is a good market for *grand cru* clarets, and growers and shippers have been tempted into selling them as soon as they are drinkable rather than wait until they are at their best. This is no doubt blameworthy, but it is certainly understandable. Every vintage which is being kept and not turned into money represents a very large capital sum tied up. Fine clarets are already dear; if a perfectionist policy were followed by growers and shippers, they would have to be a great deal dearer. The barrels in which the wine is matured cost less than ten shillings before 1914, and not much more between the wars: they now cost over ten pounds, and that fabulous rise in cost is fairly representative. The truth is that whether they like it or not the producers of fine wines are forced to turn their money over faster than they used to do.

A final note on claret dates: the region over which Bordeaux red wines are produced is not so large that there are significant climatic differences in any one year from vineyard to vineyard, so that the above rather rough guide is applicable not only to Médocs but to all red Bordeaux. However, it does sometimes happen, by some freak of what growers call the micro-climate—that is the climate considered for a single vineyard or small part of a vineyard—that a single wine will be good in a year when others are poor.

*   *   *   *   *

If you return south-west from the Médoc, back into Bordeaux, cross the river and the middle of the Entre-deux-mers triangle and carry on up to and over the Dordogne at Libourne, you will again be in claret country. Leave it on your left for the time being, and from Libourne continue eastward, following the lovely valley of the Dordogne, towards Bergerac, an agreeable small town, quiet and com-placent. From some experience of this country a curious, indeed a mysterious, rule emerges: if you stay in a small town ending in -ac you will be well lodged, exquisitely fed, and only reasonably charged.

Wherever you stay, your object should be the upper reaches of the valley, farther west, where it becomes a sort of riverine plain between cliffs honeycombed with caves. Apart from the fascination of the painted caves at Lascaux and Les Eyzies, this whole country is fine walking. Botan-ists can find the lizard orchid and many other plants of dis-tinction, for example a white asphodel. There are tiny, ancient villages, at least one of which is built into the remains of a vast monastery. And for drinking there is a wine not from the famous wine country farther west but the golden Montbazillac. Moreover, from this tranquil and well-found centre, with its alluvial soil worked by teams of small, brown oxen and a rich, sensibly backward subsis-tence economy, one of the most famous 'sights' in south-western France is not so very far away. This is Rocamadour, on its steep hill, the twelfth-century castle, not a ruin but almost intact, commanding tremendous views, its palatial fourteenth-century bishopric, its shrine to which pilgrims still resort in numbers.

On the way back (for I suggest that we are now bound for the Loire), go north from Les Eyzies to Perigeux, another plump and smiling town—as well as it may be, having been enriched by the canning of Perigord truffles— and thence through Mussidan to Coutras. Between Coutras and Libourne, in the tip of the triangle formed by the rivers Isle and Dordogne, lies Pomerol and to the east of it St. Emilion, while north-west, across the Isle, is more wine country, the Côtes de Blaye.

The inclusion of all the Gironde wines, taking in those

from the three regions named above, in the Bordeaux wines section of the *Appellation Controllée* system did not come about until 1935, but all the wines of this country are now under the rule, with its duties and obligations. And this is perhaps the place to add one note to what we have said by way of explanation of that order of merit. Although the list of *grands crus* wines (Appendix I) was originally really an order of merit, by crystallizing, as explained, into a rigid rule of definitions of wine it has to some extent changed its nature. The wines of St. Emilion, like those of the Médoc and other regions of the Bordelais vineyard, are placed, as to quality, in what is not so much a class system but a caste system. For whereas in a class system it is possible for the lower classes to work their way into the higher, in a caste system this is not possible. I have already mentioned that the wines are either *grand crus, crus bourgeois* or *artisan*. Upper-class wines, middle-class wines or working-class wines. Fortunately there is no obligation to stay within one's class when drinking them, however. The point to be repeated is that a château wine may be classed as *artisan* or *bourgeois*. The most one can say of it is that it will be good of its kind.

Seven parishes of St. Emilion have the right to their own *Appellation*, and there are two Fronsacs, between St. Emilion and Pomerol, Pomerol itself, and finally, across the Isle, three *communes* of Blaye. The latter, the Côtes wines, are considered less excellent than the St. Emilions and the Pomerols.

The centre for the region is St. Emilion itself, a small, hilly, noisy but agreeable town which exists by and for wine. True, it has an ancient and singular church worth a visit. But its real distinction is that the vines flow down to its foot like a flood of wine *in potentia*.

CHAPTER FOUR

THE LOIRE

BLAYE — Royan — Rochefort — La Rochelle — Nantes.
The coastal scenery and configuration is diverse. La
Rochelle, the greatest Protestant city in France, for all
it is a port, has no beach, a blessing since it has saved the
place from becoming a holiday-resort and it has retained its
integrity as a prosperous working town. But go as far
north as La Baule on the estuary and it is nothing *but* beach,
a holiday resort with the flimsy look of such places—that
look which threatens to turn squalid at the first touch of
failure or unpopularity, and . . . sand. La Baule, like about
twenty other places on the Atlantic coast of Europe and the
west coast of Italy, claims to have the greatest extent of sand
in our continent. It certainly has too much to be swept away
by the Walrus's forty maids with forty mops. There are
other, less popular and much pleasanter holiday resorts up
and down the coast, and many small towns with small,
welcoming hotels where, as throughout the province of
Touraine, the food is as good as the French spoken by the
cook—and that is the best. It is a pity that La Rochelle is
really too far south for the convenience of the Loire wine
visitor: certainly it is not as conventionally agreeable a
town as Nantes, but it is interesting in a manner less familiar.
It has, for about a thousand years and probably longer, been
a haven, and it has played a considerable part in France's
maritime history, especially in the very beginning. The first
of all the European colonizing ventures started not from
some Portuguese harbour, as is generally claimed, but from
La Rochelle, when Jean de Bethencourt set out to conquer
the Canary Islands in 1402. And then the town is so utterly
what the French, with apparent tautology, call a *ville*

bourgeoise, expressing something quite specific but none the less hard to define, the middle-classness, the burgher prosperity which is so striking a feature, albeit with a different face, of Tours, farther upriver.

From Nantes to Angers, Tours and Orleans is about the most fatly satisfying, and in places the loveliest, countryside in Europe, not excluding England. This, of course, is the 'châteaux country', but the châteaux have not made it; rather were they set there because the country offered so many beautiful sites in such rich land. The long chain of castles and great houses is threaded on the Loire, each dominating some gentle or glorious or spectacular view of plump, alluvial farmland, hills, woods, vineyards and river meadows.

All this has been wine country, however, since long before the châteaux were built. The first clear mention of winegrowing in the Loire valley does not occur until Merovingian times, but then in such terms that it is clear that the vineyards had been firmly established for many generations. And it stands to reason that if, as we shall see, there is proof positive of wine-growing as far north as Trèves in Lorraine and in the region of Paris by A.D. 300, then certainly this most profitable way of exploiting suitable land would have been applied farther south, and on a river which offered a perfect means of communication and freight-carrying.

Gregory of Tours—he was bishop of that city—in his *History of the Franks* has a good deal to say about the local viticulture: there are vineyards throughout his diocese; the damage to grapes caused by bad weather in the autumn is a public calamity. But most interesting of all, Gregory describes how, almost every year during the reigns of Kings Chilperic, Gontran and Childebert II, the fierce Bretons— the wild Welsh of France—raided Nantes, centre of the Loire wine trade, for the sole purpose of capturing the ripe grapes of the surrounding vineyards. In one such raid described in detail and which may be taken as typical, the Breton chieftain, Waroch by name, was able to hold the country long enough to enable his men to gather the grapes and press them. Thereafter he retreated, carrying the new wine with him into the fastnesses of Brittany. Later, again, we have evidence of a different use made of Loire wines: St. Columban, who set out for Ireland from Nantes, in A.D. 610, was able to stock up with sacramental and table wines in that city.

There is, in short, every reason to suppose that a wine-making industry was established in the Loire basin not later than about A.D. 300 and probably earlier. I shall have more to say about this later in the chapter, when we can consider a different kind of evidence.

There is a curiosity of history to be found in the names of the two principal varieties of ancient grape-vines—both *cépages nobles*—still in use among the wine-growing peasantry: the *Auvernat* and the *Breton*. That these names are old we know from the facts that the first is used in medieval legal documents, the earliest extant being dated 1302; and the second mentioned by Rabelais in *Gargantua*. As regards the *Auvernat* it may be very much older than that, however, for archeological evidence proves that there was trade between Nantes and the Auvergne quite early in the Roman Imperial period. And authorities have suggested that the *Auvernat* was one of the vines borrowed by the people of the Loire from those of a more favourable climate when they decided to try growing grapes and making wine in their own country. In short, the *Auvernat* vine is as old as the Loire wine industry, or at least its name is.

But the case of the vine called *Breton* is not so simple: it is regarded as out of the question that any vine of such high-quality fruit should have come from Brittany. Neither the climate nor the inhabitants were of a kind to produce such a variety, even supposing them to have had any vines at all; and they would hardly have raided Nantes to steal the grapes if they had. And Rabelais has something to the purpose about that. 'The good Breton wine', he says, 'grows not in Brittany, but in the good country of Verron.' It looks rather as if the Loire grew and made the wine and the Bretons traded in it.

The *Auvernat* vine was not, of course, deliberately brought from Auvergne with a view to starting a vineyard. The 'borrowing' occurred in stages. The vine is really the famous and very ancient Pinot, of Burgundian provenance;

in the thirteenth century the Orléanais called it *auvernat*— indicating that they had begun to plant it by extending into their own country the vineyards about St. Pourcain-sur-Sioule, the most northerly of the Auvernat wine-growing towns and from which they had long imported wine by way of the river. At the same period the people of Tours called this same vine *Orléans*—indicating that they had it from that city's countryside. It is in this manner that vines, and for that matter other fruit plants, 'migrate' across country.

As for the *Breton* vine, it is unquestionably a strain of the equally famous Cabernet vine of the Bordeaux region and it had obviously 'migrated' north in much the same way. Its name, in short, had in this case nothing to do with its place of origin but came from the name of the wine made from it, trade in which was centred in Nantes.

The wines of the Loire can be set in three major groups: there is a fourth, but so far away towards the source that I prefer to deal with it separately. Within the three groups the individual wines are numerous and very diverse. Beginning in the west, there is Muscadet, named not for a province but for a vine variety, like many of the wines of Alsace. This vine is, in name at least, Burgundian, *Muscadet de Bourgogne*. Yet its bearing and its grapes and the wine made from them are so different towards the mouth of the Loire, that I have sometimes wondered whether the ampelographists[1] might be mistaken as to its identity.

At all events, of the two vines chiefly planted in the west Loire vineyards, one is called *muscadet de Bourgogne*, which will serve to introduce a digression on the nomenclature of vines. This is in such a state of total confusion that it will certainly never be reduced to order unless by some learned German or American willing to devote an entire lifetime of patient work to the task. No Frenchman of our time would dream of spending time on it. There are probably something

---

[1] An ampelographist is a student—or a professor for that matter—of the morphology and behaviour of the vine. The word comes from *ampelidae*, formerly the name of the family of plants to which the genus *Vitis* belongs, some others of which family also produce edible fruits, although they have never been brought into cultivation. This name, botanists have amused themselves by changing to *Vitacae;* perhaps the man who used to be an ampelographist is now a vitaegraphist or some such word.

like seven thousand varietal names, and possibly many
more; there are probably about three thousand *cépages* in
cultivation somewhere, but it may possibly really be many
fewer. In short, there are several names, sometimes many,
for every variety. But no sooner is it decided that two names
really belong to one variety than some trifling difference in
behaviour makes this doubtful. And the simple reason is
that growers, when propagating a variety, choose a parent
vine from which to take scions which has qualities of local
value, so that there is a constant slow creation if not of new
varieties, at least of new *clones*. Moreover, the vine 'sports'
quite readily. Syrah, one of the most famous of the *Cépages
nobles*, the noble varieties which yield fine wine, has produced an astonishing number of mutations. I myself have a
Pinot Meunier which is morphologically indistinguishable
from others of that name, whether in England, where it
has been established since about A.D. 300, or in France.
Yet this strain of the variety ripens fruit ten days ahead of
the 'standard' Pinot Meunier, a quality of very great value in
England, or in northern France for that matter; a strain of
Early Pinot Meunier is being developed from this mutant,
by propagation. Again, the variety Gamay Hatif des Vosges
is not one of the great Gamay family at all. On the other
hand, some so-called Madeleines are *really* Chardonnays.
It is a nightmare. The greatest work of ampelography ever
written is that of Viala and Vermorel; it consists of accurate drawings and careful descriptions of varieties of the
vine in cultivation half-way through the nineteenth century; it is in eleven enormous volumes and it is nothing like
complete. Since its publication there have been hundreds of
ampelographies published in twenty countries, and scores
of treatises on ampelographical method. But disorder con-
tinues to reign, and any enthusiast with an eye for the shape
of a leaf, the 'carriage' of a plant, the delicacy or otherwise
of a tendril, can spot aliens among the vines of the most
sacredly *controllée* vineyards of every *Appellation d'Origine*
region.

My own belief, based on a little practical experience—to
wit the tending of a couple of thousand vines for ten years
—is that vines are so flexible that they tend to change their

qualities to suit a new soil and climate. And as the most locally suitable plants are selected for propagating, new varieties are developed out of old ones in every generation. If this be true, then the Muscadet of the Loire may look like its Burgundian ancestor, but it need not produce identical grapes.

The second Loire vine region is Anjou, and in this case the wines bear a place-name, as usual farther south, not a vine-name, as usual in the north-east. And the third region is that of Vouvray, again a place-name wine. Within and between these three are rather numerous wines with strong individual qualities; notably for my taste the wines of Saumur, one of the pleasantest of the Loire towns. It was there, in a restaurant overlooking the river much frequented by officers of the garrison and—always a sign of a good pub in France—by the more prosperous commercial travellers, that I first drank Brèzé, a white wine which sparkles not in the ostentatious manner of champagne but with restraint. Such wines are described as *légèrement petillant*; there is no English for this but what it expresses is a sort of chuckling liveliness rather than the pushing exuberance of champagne.

The tendency of Loire wines to become slightly effervescent after they have apparently stopped fermenting and settled down is said to be one of the reasons why they are not better known in England. Wines imported in the wood and bottled over here pay less duty than wines imported in bottle. Why, heaven knows; it is just one of those whimsicalities which suggest that the Customs and Excise department is staffed by the last of the English eccentrics. As most English wine-drinkers will pay a highish price only for wines they have known by name for most of their lives, importing Loire wines in bottle means pricing them out of the market. But if they are imported in the wood, all but a few of the best shippers bottle them too soon, before they have got over their journey and settled down again. This has unhappy consequences.

There is a great deal of controversy about these secondary ferments, which occur not only in Loire wines but in many others. In some cases they are true wine-yeast ferments due to the continued presence of sugar in the wine,

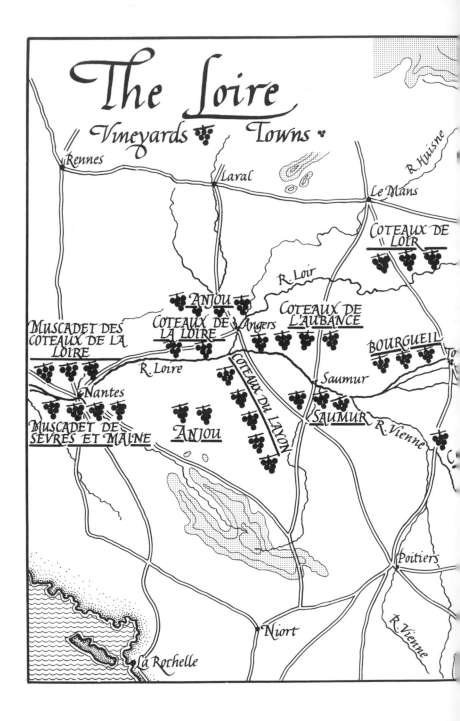

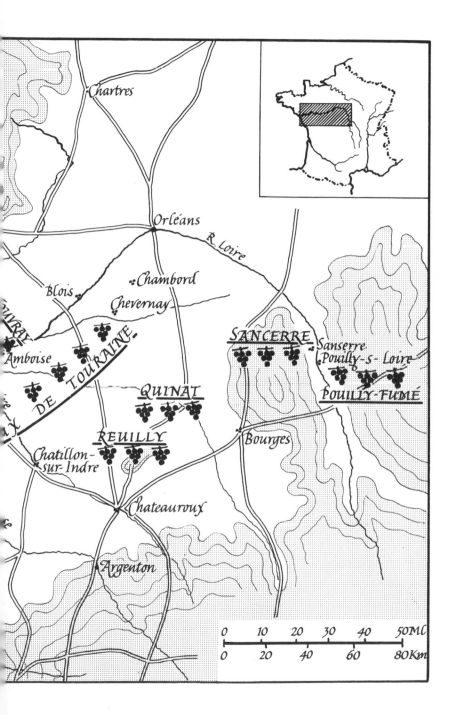

and some disturbance such as a rise in temperature. But in other cases the ferment may be of a different kind; this is the malo-lactic ferment, the consequence of which is a lowering of acidity in the wine as malo-lactic acid is eaten up by the active organism. Vintners who welcome this lowering of acidity, notably the highly scientific wine-makers of Switzerland and their academic advisers, hold that no wine is complete until it has undergone this ferment, and that the ferment should, if necessary, be provoked. However, vintners whose wine has just the acidity they want, regard the malo-lactic ferment as a disaster, and as a disease of wine. At all events, whether the ferment in this case is a secondary sugar ferment, as seems likely, or a malo-lactic ferment, its consequence is that the English visitor to the Loire will have a chance to taste many wines he has not heard of, and very fine some of them are.

The vineyards about Nantes are stocked either with Muscadet, synonym Melon, or with Gros Plant, which has half a dozen synonyms. These are used either unblended or blended in the wine-making. The vineyard holdings both here and upriver are for the most part small, some of them very small, and worked by proprietors who have a regular job in some other trade, just as many builders, carpenters, garage-owners and others in East Kent own a piece of cherry orchard or half an acre of strawberries. Muscadet wines are full in a hot year, light and delicate in a moderate year, their alcohol content varying from as low as 9°, in which case they are not allowed to be sold under the *Appellation Controllée* label, to as much as 13°, in which case they may be very long-lived. On the whole, however, Muscadet is drunk young; I once asked a Nantais cellarer for how long his wine improved with keeping. He said that, with freakish exceptions, no Loire wine improved in bottle after three years, and that in most years it could and should be drunk the year following the vintage. He added, *sotto voce* and perhaps with his fingers crossed, that in his opinion no white wine in the world got any benefit from more than three years in bottle. I do not know enough about it to pass judgement on this opinion.

The whole of the Loire vineyard being relatively northerly for the vine, the quality of the wine varies greatly from year to year, with the weather, which is thoroughly unreliable. A point here which is usually missed: a really wet, cool summer not only means one bad vintage, it often means two, however fine the weather in the following year. The reason is that the vine depends on the sun not only to ripen its grapes but also its wood, for if the wood does not lignify well, and it does not in cold, wet weather, there will be little fruit in the following season. Although, in choosing the *cépages* for a given region, the wood-ripening propensity of the varieties is taken into account, it is a very secondary consideration to the quality of the grapes. Consequently, by an unfortunate genetical attribute of the species, a variety with very fine grapes may have bad habits in the matter of ripening its wood; the two things are not genetically linked excepting in a few of the newest hybrids which have not yet received the accolade of nobility.

The Loire valley is apt to suffer from wet summers; in such years the wines are, in my view, poor. Light white wines are very dependent for their character on nose; it is sun which makes nose; no sun, no bouquet; no bouquet, no character. Muscadet of a good year is a wholly delicious wine; in a bad year it is . . . just wine. The better sort of merchants hold stocks of good years to blend with poor years, thus producing an excellent standard product.

If you are in Nantes, the first of the major châteaux to be visited—but as a 'sight', not a vineyard—is the ducal castle in Nantes itself, formerly the home of the Breton sovereigns. The cathedral, for those who collect Gothic, is a very fine specimen, although all its glass was destroyed by, I think, our own or American bombing of the kind we took for granted as necessary at the time, although as a matter of fact it did nothing whatever to forward our victory, embittered the French, and was the product of nothing excepting the serious want of ideas which inflicts professional military men. To me Nantes cathedral seems a more integral, of-a-piece, work of art than Reims, as compact and graspable as Canterbury, and almost as graceful, but not quite, as Salisbury.

It is easy to arrange with the Nantes *syndicat d'initiative* to visit some of the principal *caves*. In the larger ones much wine is fermented and matured in concrete vats lined with glass. The more conservative, and in my view conscientious, vintners, use barrels: wine needs oak, no matter what the worshippers of hygiene may say. If you are able to do some tasting in the cellars and that is, or should be, the object of your visit, you will find a difference between Muscadet and Gros Plant wines, the latter being notably dry. The local people, and they should know, make a distinction, moreover, between two major Muscadet groups; there is Muscadet des Coteaux de la Loire; and Muscadet de Sevre-et-Maine. This is valid and recognized by the authorities, so that these two names are two different *Appellations*. I did not myself find it easy to make the distinction, and it was admitted to me that where the soil of one region is virtually the same as that of another, as may happen in some vineyards, the wines are indeed very much alike.

The drive from Nantes to Angers is through country so lovely that it has all the air of a work of art by a considerable, although conventional, genius. And of course it is, to some extent, an artefact, for it has been worked over by man for a couple of thousand years. The valleys are intensively cultivated and stocked. Above the bottoms, where small, neat villages form centres for each area of fat farming land, the lower slopes of the valley sides are planted to vines; above the vines the hills are well-wooded. The whole landscape is plump and shapely, although farther upriver there is a note of more rugged grandeur introduced by the huge rocky outcrop of the Mont. The châteaux, crowning their hilltops, occur at the correct intervals for the pleasure of the eye, and are so various in style, due to diversity of age, that they are a kind of social history of the last four centuries, done in stone. The riverine scenery differs from our own in that the trees are planted with more regularity, an error of taste, but economically sound; and the smaller gardens have more to offer the palate and the stomach than the eye. Those larger gardens which *are* ornamental have that tiresome stylized regularity which to the subtler eye of the English gardener is a horticultural bore. But perhaps— though I can never resist doing it—it is as much a mistake

to try comparing English and French gardens, as to compare the regular tramp of Racine's verse with the dance of
Shakespeare's. The French make only one aesthetic mistake,
but they make it all the time: they equate elegance with
strict rules. At all events, Angers castle has one of these
French gardens. The castle itself is a medieval fortress.
They do not interest me, so I did not visit it. However, in a
brand-new wing necessitated by more of that rather wild
bomb-slinging animadverted on above, there is a remarkable work of tapestry to be seen, the tapestry of the Apoca-
lypse, made in the fourteenth century. There is also an open-
air theatre to be visited if you happen to be in Angers during
the annual July drama festival.

The wines of Anjou are white, red and *rosé*. The best are
white, but the *rosé* are better known, at least in England.
Anjous have four *Appellations*: Coteaux de l'Aubance;
Coteaux du Layon: these are full, sometimes sweet white
wines notable for their bouquet in good years. Also famous
for nose are, thirdly, Coteaux de la Loire, wines grown on
the slopes of the main stream's right bank. Farther east upriver are Coteaux de Saumur wines, which I prefer to the rest.

The Angevins must, during their century or so of common citizenship with the English, who were locally known
as the *goddams*—which proves that military swearing evolves
from the blasphemous to the obscene—have acquired a
measure of Anglo-Saxon whimsicality and poetry. For
whereas the Bordelais discuss wine as it is, complain bit-
terly of the taxes they brilliantly evade, and explain why it is
that nobody ever makes a penny out of wine-growing while
offering you a lift in their three-million-franc American car
at the same time, the Angevins will, if not firmly discour-
aged, tell you charming tales of the origins of viticulture in
their country. They *are* charming, and can be listened to
with great pleasure after a pint of Saumur; they are also
nonsensical. For example, the well-known story about the
value of hard pruning being discovered following the eating
down of the vineyard full of vines by some ecclesiastic's
straying ass. However, there is always something quite local
about pruning and cultivating techniques, for this reason:
that when a region is newly planted to vines it is usually

necessary to experiment with half a dozen or more ways of pruning the plants to discover which yields the best results. And it takes more than an ass to discover it. The techniques of grafting, pruning and cultivating generally had certainly all been discovered and tried in the highly sophisticated civilization of Egypt not later than 1200 B.C. The Romans knew them all. The early French viticulteurs had nothing much to discover; they had only to modify immemorial traditional usages. Even the rather self-conscious jolliness about wine which is part of the mystique of Anjou, as of Beaujolais, is ancient Egyptian: 'The mouth of a happy man is filled with wine' would do very well for a wine-growers' co-operative poster, but is in fact an old wine-cellar inscription from Memphis. I myself came across a minor example of this nothing-new-under-the-vineyard-sun business. There is a method of pruning vines in northerly vineyards, for high quality in the harvest, called after Dr. Jules Guyot, who devised it. (Dr. Guyot was the greatest of nineteenth-century French pomologists.) But his method had been in use in English vineyards in the sixteenth and seventeenth centuries, and John Rose, Charles II's gardener, whose treatise on vineyards Dr. Guyot had certainly never read, describes it exactly.

The villages about Angers, as indeed through the Touraine, are famous for the neat prettiness of their houses and gardens, and the innkeepers for the excellence of their cooking.

The white wines of Anjou are made from a Pinot grape, the vine being called Auvernat, Pinot blanc, or Pinot de la Loire. It is related to the Burgundian Pinots, which are also planted in Champagne. The family of the Pinots is an ancient and rather primitive one, and may well have been grown in Anjou since the third century. Its ancestors include some of the very early cultivated varieties of the Caucasus, introduced by way of Greece and Italy; and also wild French vines. (This pedigree has been established by Dr. Negrul at the Leningrad Academy of Applied Botany, if that be the correct translation of its name.) The *vin rosé* of Anjou comes from Cabernet Sauvignon, a cross between two of the noblest *cépages* in France.

I am frequently surprised to hear two businessmen sitting down to luncheon in a London restaurant, assuring each other that it is too hot for a substantial wine when there is work to be done that afternoon, and ordering a bottle, or rather a carafe, of *rosé*. Certainly a *rosé looks* lighter than a red wine, and sometimes it may actually *be* lighter. It is quite as often nothing of the sort. At least one *rosé* much drunk in London, and of which more anon, is a terribly quarrelsome wine, and has no doubt been responsible for many an abortive deal. Now if you plant Cabernet Sauvignon in sand or gravel you get, in all but heat-wave years, a light wine which would not hurt a child. But as there is a great demand for this wine it is grown where room can be found, sometimes in massive clay, and in that case it produces, in fine years, a very strongly alcoholic wine which is not, in my opinion, at all good for the liver. And not very nice anyway. However, if you like *rosé*, and it can be very pleasant, do not buy it in a carafe but in a bottle with a label marked *Appellation Controllée*, in which case the chances are that the wine was grown in a light, stony soil and the wine itself should be light, fragrant, not excessively alcoholic; admirable for elevenses.

Anjou red wines come from Cabernet franc vines (Breton) and are sound without being of any particular interest. The best come from Champigny.

The visitor should be in no hurry to leave Angers. It is one of the pleasantest towns in France and a convenient centre from which to visit about a dozen famous châteaux, some of them, like Brissac, in the Côteaux de l'Aubance *Appellation*, being wine châteaux. Its white wine, like several others in this part of the country, while it is usually drunk young, is capable in good years of surprising longevity: twenty-five years is not unusual, and one or two of the best years have been excellent at fifty. At that age the wine will have darkened in colour until a glass of it looks like a big amber bead; it pours slow and heavy from the bottle and is of extraordinary fragrance.

Between Angers and Saumur you are again, as on the most interesting reaches of the Dordogne, in a country whose flat and gently sloping river valley is contained by cliffs.

The rock faces of the Loire are full of caves which, like those of the Dordogne, may conceivably have been used as prehistoric dwellings. Whether or not they housed the ancient Tourangeaux, they certainly house the modern ones, but nowadays the caves have all the amenities of masonry fronts, doors and windows. The caves are both houses and wine-cellars, and have the advantage of a perfectly even temperature throughout the year, whatever the season or the weather.

Saumur is a cavalry regiment garrison town and is consequently very high-toned. The people are almost as well bred as the horses, if they still have any horses, and the wine has the same refined elegance concealing great strength, as a blood horse. Horsiness prevails, and Saumur château, dominating town, river and countryside from its height, should be visited by all horse-lovers, for it has a museum devoted to equitation and the horse which is, as far as I know, unique in the world. The members of your party not interested in horses can sit and drink one of the dry, brisk wines of the Saumurois without taking any harm, for they are as well mannered as any wines in Europe.

The town of Tours on a Saturday afternoon is the living explanation of how and why France survives its wretched governments: and also perhaps why those governments are as bad as they are. The French really are a freedom-loving people and far too logical to confuse, as we do, the freedom of great national strength, which entails a measure of bondage for the individual, and real, personal freedom. They keep their governments as weak as possible, for they know instinctively that strong government inevitably means bondage for the citizen. They have, of course, overdone it: the contempt in which politics and politicians are held has reduced France as a nation to semi-impotence. It has left the French people, as distinct from the political entity called France, still the freest and most complete human beings in the world. Tours, then, is *fat*: the sheer, complacent fleshiness of the place, the costly soundness of building, furniture, clothes; the vigorous health of the people, all these compose a picture of thriving middle-class prosperity. The English were once called a nation of shop-keepers; it must have been a mistake for shop-stewards. Compare the number and quality of shops in France with our own, and it will at once be apparent which people make the keenest and best shop-keepers. France is as middle class, her people as ruthlessly insistent on their comforts and as unwaveringly acquisitive, as the English are essentially proletarian . . . unthrifty, diffident about personal rights, and relatively submissive to authority.

The wine town of the Tours region is Vouvray, and there is no small town in the world better pleased with itself, nor with better reason to be so. Vouvray is on the Loire east of Tours. Its opposite number across the river is Montlouis, half a mile away over water, but ten miles by road since there is no bridge. Go from Tours to Montlouis, thence to Amboise, and double back to Vouvray.

The white wines of the reach between Tours and Montlouis are made from Pinot blanc (Auvernat) grapes cultivated by a people of ancient race. Many of them live in chalk-cliff caves, others in the prettiest, most completely bucolic villages of France. Their wines are even more remarkable for longevity in great years than those which come from farther downstream. There is said, but I have never tasted it and am never likely to, to be some of the 1834 still in being and still exquisite. Presumably 1834 was, like 1921, a summer of unbroken sunshine for six months. According to the records, the 1870 was another such wine. The Montlouis wines of ordinary years, such as we the common drinkers can buy, are very good, very pleasant, but not outstanding for character. Nowhere, excepting beyond what is regarded as the northern limit for vine cultivation, does the weather make so much difference to the wine of the year, for in Alsace, and on the Rhine generally, the weather is more steadily 'continental' and less subject to the whimsicalities of the Atlantic influence. However, the better Montlouis, like the better wines of the *Vieux Comté Nantais*, are blended of good and indifferent years, and a standard of quality can be relied upon.

The château of Amboise, on the way from Montlouis to Vouvray, should be visited after reading its history, although architecturally it is as interesting as it is historically, for it is apparently the origin of the whole Loire version of Renaissance style, a style acquired in Italy by the men of taste who, no doubt, were to be found in the armies of Charles VIII and Francis I. Armies invading Italy are always apt to get themselves conquered not by the soldiers but by the beauty of that country. The Italy which the French invaded at the beginning of the sixteenth century was the Italy which can best be recaptured by reading the *Memoirs* of Benvenuto Cellini, a land of tiny, warring, striving, city states whose most ruffianly leaders, churchmen or soldiers, were all passionately interested in the arts; and whose exuberant citizens were all busily engaged either in cutting each other's throats or in creating objects of beauty, from jewels to great houses and churches. This was the influence under which Amboise and the châteaux of the Loire were built or partially rebuilt. But Loire Renaissance is no more a mere copy of the Italian *cinquocento* than English Palladian is a mere copy of an Italian style. And there is much interest in comparing what the French made of Italian building styles with what the English made of them a century or a century and a half later.

For some reason or other—one might make a guess at it—the people of Vouvray are inordinately proud of their sparkling white wines. Monsieur Charles Vavasseur, *viticulteur* and former mayor of the *commune*, made the claim that these wines are as good as the best champagnes, and this claim has become common form in the town. It is quite possibly true; it is quite certainly true that not one person in fifty thousand could distinguish a sparkling Vouvray from a good champagne of equal sweetness or dryness. Personally I have a blind spot: I cannot see that this is anything to boast about because I do not find it possible to attribute to sparkling wines any of those qualities of character which distinguish good, still wines. There are, of course, nasty sour sparkling wines, and there are disgustingly sweet ones which taste about as interesting as fizzy lemonade. Champagnes do not descend to those depths, and nor do sparkling Vouvrays. But even the best champagnes are, in my opinion, neutral, a fact which the bubbles, stinging the palate, serve to disguise. I propose to enlarge on that oenological heresy when we get to Champagne. Meanwhile, let it be said that Vouvray has quite enough sound, still wine to be proud of without having to boast of its *mousseux*.

Vouvray and its environs had the honour of being described by one of the greatest of French novelists, for more than one of Balzac's characters went there, and if I remember rightly, the Illustrious Gaudissart was a native. 'The village of Vouvray', Balzac says, 'is bedded among the gorges and outcrops of its own rocky massif, the cliff of rock which begins to form an elbow of the river below the bridge at Cisse. From Vouvray to Tours the startling anfractuosities of this same rugged hill system are inhabited by a people of vine-growers. In more than one place there are houses on three different levels, cut into the living rock and connected by stairways hacked out of the native stone.'

Balzac goes on to describe how, owing to this building in the vertical instead of the horizontal plane, the smoke of one man's kitchen fire may emerge between the stocks of another man's vineyard, and he describes the fields and vineyards as *perpendicular*. They are not quite that, but it is this very steep sloping of the land that gives the wine its quality. The vines are tipped towards the sun and protected from the colder quarters, and such siting may make as much as a month's difference to the ripening time, and therefore ultimate maturity, of the grapes. Growing vines in such conditions is like growing grapes on a wall.

The named wines of Vouvray come not from '*châteaux*', but, as in Burgundy, from '*clos*'. A *clos* is, literally, an enclosure, and the word in this context refers to a walled holding or farm. Typical of the Vouvrois *clos* is the *Clos de l'Epinay*, formerly the property of the duc de Choiseul. There is a fine manor-type farmhouse in one corner, a few trees, and for the rest several thousand symmetrically planted vines, the whole enclosed by a handsome wall coped with tiles.

The whole region, albeit densely populated—the Loire is viticultural ribbon-development—offers fine, diverse walking, or rather, in some places at least, scrambling, with delightful views of the river and its banks, extending sometimes as far as Tours downstream and Amboise upstream.

Gregory of Tours, who was writing the history we have already referred to in the fourth quarter of the sixth century, says that the first vineyard in the Vouvray region was planted on the Marmoutiers slopes by St. Martin in the fourth quarter of the fourth century. It is a fact that St. Martin is regarded locally as the originator and patron saint of Loire viticulture, but it is more likely that if there was a fourth-century planting it was a new beginning, a reintroduction of the vine to those slopes, for it has probably, as we have already seen, been cultivated in parts of the Loire valley since the second century. There was the edict of the emperor Domitian, already referred to, that all the vineyards, with some special exceptions in the east, within the Empire and outside Italy, were to be grubbed up. And we know that it was not officially reversed until A.D. 280 in the reign of the emperor Probus. St. Martin's planting was, perhaps, the first after this new and more liberal policy towards the provinces had been adopted by the imperial government's ministry of agriculture.

Parts of the Loire valley still had their primaeval forest cover as late as the early Middle Ages. It was the monks of the various and populous monastic houses who finally cleared the trees and planted crops, including vines. Roman ploughs had never been much good for that kind of work; the heavier soils had to wait for the eight-ox German plough of the kind the Saxons used to break the Kentish Weald. There was not much land of that kind on the Loire, certainly, but no doubt the 'anfractuosities' referred to by Balzac were equally discouraging. At all events the majority of what are now the best wine slopes were first cleared of trees and planted to vines between the eighth and twelfth centuries. At the present time the whole vineyard area is broken up into small holdings, which gives diversity to the cultivated landscape and accounts for the populousness of the region.

One step ahead of the English owners of stately homes who have taken to showing them to visitors for half a crown a head, the French owners of Loire châteaux devised the now famous *Son et Lumière* type of spectacle which has added a tourist amenity to the region. The nearest *Son et*

Lumière show to Vouvray is, I think, at Chenonceaux. For those who have never seen one of these dramatizations by recorded voice and music, and by floodlighting skilfully managed, of a great house's history, the spectacle is worth seeing. It is usually claimed that owing to the natural excellence of French taste these shows are free from vulgarity. Why anyone bothers to protest about it I cannot imagine: the whole *Son et Lumière* stunt is splendidly vulgar, and the former tenants of the castles thus displayed for our admiration would have sent the present owners and all the visitors, paying or not, to the Bastille. *Son et Lumière* at Chenonceaux is striking and curious and should be seen and heard.

Of the other Touraine wines, two are entitled to their own *Appellation d'Origine*, they are those of Chinon and of Bourgeuil. Chinon vineyards centre on the ruined castle of that name. It is an ancient one, for Joan of Arc there launched the campaign to detach the Loire provinces from the English crown, an act which the British government have been resenting ever since by over-taxing wine imports. The one really desirable consequence which might have been expected from the war did not happen: English viticulture continued to decline instead of rising to new heights.

Chinon and Bourgeuil wines are identical, only it is best not to say so when you are visiting the two places concerned, since the local experts claim to tell t'other from which. The best are the reds and they are very pleasant wines which we should know better. They are, unhappily, not perfectly stable: they are apt, when taken in the wood from their cool cellars, to start fermenting again in transit, which probably accounts for their being so little known. Oddly enough I have found myself preferring Bourgeuils of an only moderate year to those of the best years; I think the reason is that these wines cannot 'carry' the high alcohol content of very good years; they become too heady. They are essentially light wines. However, they are said to vary according to the vineyard soil, some being from limestone gravel and some from sand. It should be said that I have very little experience of these wines and it is very likely that mine came from the 'wrong' kind of soil. Also the wine I had may have been too young for the vintage: the good years are said to need five years ageing, and can stand ten years.

There are two other small groups of wines which the all-powerful *Comité National des Appellations d'Origine des Vins et Eaux-de-vie*—CNAO for short—place under the general heading *Loire*, presumably because the vineyards in question are in fact on that river. But they are so much nearer the source than the mouth that they are in quite another part of France, in the Jura, and I prefer to visit them when we get nearer to that part of the country.

So . . . from Tours, follow the river to Orleans, which is a good jumping-off place for almost anywhere in France.

CHAPTER FIVE

CHAMPAGNE

ORLEANS–Paris–Reims, Reims being to champagne what Bordeaux is to claret and Lyon to burgundy. The Champagne vineyards are the most northerly in France, lying south of Reims and a little north of the 49th parallel of latitude. Even the Alsatian vineyards are a shade farther south, since they come between Strasburg and Colmar and thus lie nearer to the same parallel. The vineyards of Champagne are between 350 and 650 feet above sea-level, on a vast plain; those of Alsace, although surrounded by mountains, and in some cases planted high, are not so very much higher because the Alsatian plain east of the Vosges mountains is the bottom of a deep valley. Both regions have a 'continental' climate. Thus it is probably true to say that the grapes of Champagne are grown under less favourable conditions than anywhere else in France.

It has already been pointed out that the finest wines are made from grapes grown on the outskirts, as it were, of the principal viticultural region of Europe. They come either from high latitudes or, grown farther south, from high altitudes, as in Italy and Spain where the good wines are all mountain wines. But there is a limit to this rule: it would not be possible to produce the qualities of Bordeaux wines as far north as Reims: nor, of course, would anyone try to do so. One of the triumphs of wine-growing in its long history has been the development of those qualities in wine which a given place tends to produce, a sort of super example of making a virtue of necessity; or rather, in the case of fine wines, a *vertu*. Thus the qualities of wine grown in the north are different from and not comparable with those of southern wines. In the case of Champagne, however, I

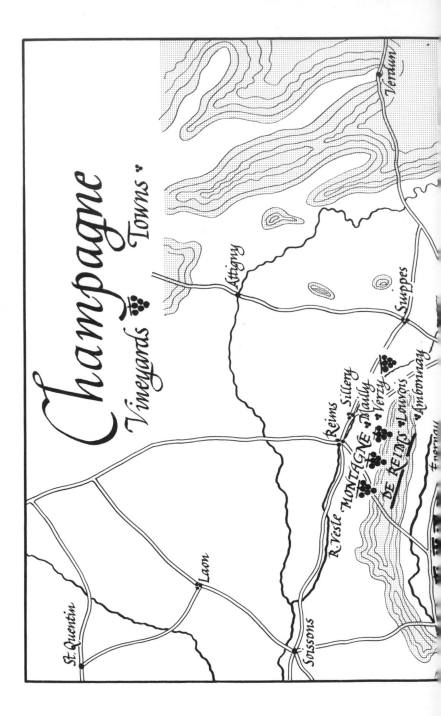

Champagne

Vineyards 🍇 Towns

St. Quentin

Laon

Soissons

Reims

Attigny

Verdun

Suippes

R. Vesle

MONTAGNE

DE REIMS

Sillery

Mailly

Verzy

Mayors

Ambonnay

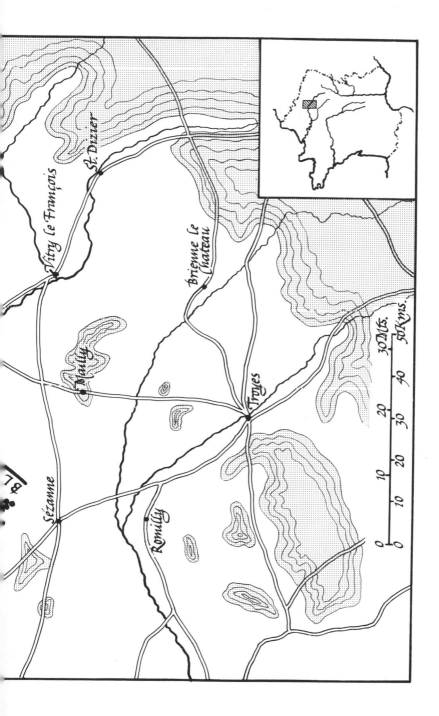

shall have to rely trustingly on other palates than my own.
I can tell a good champagne from a bad one, and that is
about as far as it goes. It is fair to add that this does not mean
I think I am right and everyone else wrong. It only means
that bubbles spoil my palate. So that in Champagne I am a
wine heretic.

The 'official' northerly limit for viticulture is 50° N. This
parallel crosses a tiny bit of England five miles north of the
Lizard Head, crosses the French coast between Tréport and
Dieppe, the Belgian frontier east of La Capelle, so that a
piece of Belgium lies to the south of it. It bisects Luxemburg with two-thirds of that small country to its south—
Luxemburg grows its own wine—and it crosses the Rhine
at Mainz. But in practice this limit is obviously somewhat
arbitrary, a sort of average. By careful choice of site and soil
and variety, vineyards can be cultivated more or less successfully at least as high as latitude 51° N. For a steep
south-facing slope sheltered by the shape of the land or by
woods from the cold quarters is warmer north of 50° N.
than an exposed position south of it. It might very well
be possible to find, north of the line, sites which would be
considerably more favourable than the famous vineyards of
Champagne which lie south of it; such was, no doubt, the
case of the Marquis of Bute's vineyard—23 acres at its
greatest in about 1875—in Glamorganshire, where the
variety grown was a Gamay neither so early nor so *hatif*
as the Pinot of Champagne. (See Chapter 7.)

The heart of the Champagne viticultural country is the
département of the *Marne.* By following the river from which
that *département* gets its name, from Château Thierry in the
west to Chalons-sur-Marne in the east, you drive—or float
if you like—through the heart of Champagne. But the wine
country sprawls, as it were; there are outlying vineyards
in the *département* of the *Aube,* the *Aisne, Seine-et-Marne* and
Haute Marne, so that in fact the vineyards whose wines are
entitled to the *Appellation Controllée Champagne* are rather
scattered and separated by country where other crops than
wine are grown. And this is partly for the reasons outlined
above: that in so northerly a province the sites for vines
must be carefully chosen.

Nor does the relatively cold climate constitute the only singularity of the Champagne province. The region is a great pan of chalk, and although excess of calcium imparts a special quality and *finesse* to white wines, it also constitutes a serious difficulty since a great many wine varieties are subject to chlorosis, an iron-deficiency disease induced by too much lime in the soil. But the fact is that the arable layer of the Champagne vineyards is an artefact, man-made over many generations by annual dressings of farmyard manure which would be excessive in more southerly vineyards, and of the special local composts which the *vignerons*, the vine-peasantry, call *magasins*, possibly because they contain a bit of everything. In some places this practice has, despite a solid and friable chalk sub-soil, reduced the calcareous content of the top-soil to no more than 20 per cent. Elsewhere it remains as high as 40 per cent.

Formerly, before the great *Phylloxera* disaster which probably cost France more than the Franco-Prussian war— and like that calamity due to an alien invader—Champagne vineyards were incredibly crowded. For various reasons it is usual for the density of plantation to increase as one moves north through Europe: the vines are pruned harder; root-competition helps to dwarf them, making them prematurely old, hard and fruitful; they keep each other warm in frosty spring weather, the sort of weather which destroys the crop in flower-bud as late as May 15 in such northerly vineyards (and even in the southerly ones in many years). Up to the end of the nineteenth century or thereabouts it would not be unusual to find as many as 16,000 vines per acre in Champagne, which must have made hoeing them extremely awkward. It was not, indeed, customary to plant more than 10,000 to the acre, but the practice of *provignage* raised and even doubled that number in course of time. *Provignage* consists in sticking the tip of a ripe vine cane into the ground while it is still attached to the parent stock, so that it forms a hoop. The tip strikes root, forming a new vine, but still attached to the old one, and in due course the new stock would have its own *provin*, and so on. A vineyard might consist of a whole series of such hooped rows, and as they were thus self-supporting they did not have to be staked, wired or tied, the fruitful shoots arising from the hoops. It is, as we shall see when we come to Burgundy, an extremely ancient method, and it is also a very good one. *Phylloxera* makes it impossible since, to survive, every vine must be grafted and a naturally struck root is at the mercy of this root aphis. Almost the only country in the temperate zones where this method might still be practised with advantage would be England, where *Phylloxera* has never contrived to establish itself although it has made several attempts to do so.

Mechanization, even in the absence of *Phylloxera*, would have made *provignage* impossible, excepting for the fact that since smallholding is the rule in most vineyard regions of France, the degree of mechanization is relatively small. But in large vineyards there must be room between the rows for tractors to pass. For this reason the rule in modern Champagne vineyards is planting at about a yard and a half 'square'. And the rows of vines are provided with stakes and wires for tying-in the fruit-bearing shoots of the year.

Before the varieties of grapes to be grown for champagne, as for other wines, were laid down by law, a considerable number of *cépages* was planted, notably various strains of Gamay. Excellent wine can be, and in places still is, made from the grapes of this ancient variety, but it fell upon evil days in the third quarter of the last century when attacked, for reasons which may or may not have been good, by the great Dr. Jules Guyot. It is no longer allowed in Champagne. I am unable to say whether the limitations imposed on choice of varieties by law were or were not of advantage to the wine, but at all events growers must now plant none but Pinots, in several strains, Arbanne and Petit Meslier. Arbanne, a variety which as far as I know is confined to the neighbourhood of Bar-sur-Aube, produces a small but very high-quality crop yielding a wine of exquisite bouquet. It is going out of cultivation as uneconomic. Petit Meslier belongs to a family of Mesliers which, when they consent to crop, ripen very well in East Kent and yield good wine there. One member of the family was at one time widely planted in New Zealand, but was so susceptible to the fungus disease *P. viticola* that the frequency of copper sprayings necessary made it too expensive to grow. Petit Meslier, peculiar to the Marne Valley about Venteuil, yielded white wines of exceptional delicacy, but it has gone out of cultivation owing to its incompatibility with so many of the suitable rootstocks, which makes growing it excessively difficult—one clear case of *Phylloxera* spoiling the quality of a wine by simply making it ungrowable!

That leaves three Pinots as the wine-grapes of Champagne. Pinot Noir and Pinot Blanc Chardonnay for the *premiers crus*, and Pinot Meunier for the second *crus*. All three are 'earlies', the only kind that can be grown in Champagne if consistent crops are wanted, which of course they are. All three, indeed, do quite well on suitable sites in southern England, and very well indeed on really favourable sites such as against a south wall or on a really steep south slope. Pinot Noir is by far the most important Champagne grape, its juice being colourless and yielding a wine of the highest quality. Pinot Meunier, burgeoning later and therefore less liable to frost damage, ripens its fruit earlier. Its wine is less acid and ages more quickly, but never quite as good. This vine is widely planted on the Marne between Epernay and Château Thierry. South of the river, in the area called the Côtes des Blancs, the vine is Chardonnay (a Pinot Blanc really) and identical with the Chardonnay of Burgundy.

There are about 42,000 acres of Champagne vineyards, and of these 15,000 are owned and cultivated by great firms with world-famous names. The remaining 27,000-odd acres are owned by no fewer than 15,000 smallholding *viticulteurs*, so that here, as in most of the other wine-growing countrysides, smallholding is predominant and many proprietors have less than one acre of vines. Smallholders and great farmers together produce about 30 million bottles of champagne a year.

Although Epernay is geographically the centre of Champagne, Reims is the city identified with the wine, not only because of its commercial importance but because in the course of building first the Roman city, later the cathedral and the medieval city, and finally in the course of winning stone for industrial purposes, quarriers cut such vast amounts of stone out of the chalk matrix of the earth—the same chalk system as Kent and Sussex—that they left tens of miles of tunnels very suitable for the storing, and some processes of the making, of champagne. It is true that the same convenience is to be found in Epernay and at Ay, but the huge output of Champagne requires as much of this accommodation as possible. From the visitor's point of view, Reims has advantages as a centre; the beauty of its great cathedral and the need to visit it often in order to see it all, is one predominant reason, sufficient in my view to give the city all the advantage it needs over Epernay, for all that it is a pleasant town enough.

Visiting the Champagne country is touring made easy, for it simply entails following the *route du Champagne*, signposted as such. However, it is not one but three *routes*, three round tours, since there are three principal areas of wine production.

1. *La Montagne de Reims*

This is sometimes called the *Côtes des Noirs* in reference to its black grapes (Pinot Noir). For tourist purposes it is called the *Blue Circuit*. It is divided into two sub-regions, the *Grande*, and the *Petite*, Mountain of Reims—any small rise of ground in this vast flat plain is apt to be called a mountain.

The *Grande Montagne* has six *grand crus* wines:

Verzy	Mailly
Verzenay	Rilly
Beaumont	Sillery

and five *premiers crus*:

Trépail	Chigny-les-Roses
Villers-Marmery	Villers-Allerand
Ludes	

The *crus* of the *Petite Montagne* are:

Chamery	Villedommange
Eceuil	Jorny
Sacy	Parguy

Between the Mountain of Reims vineyards and those of the Marne valley there is a link, the *Côte de Bouzy et d'Ambonnay*, with five *grands crus*, to wit:

Bouzy	Louvoirs
Ambonnay	Tours-sur-Marne
Tauxières	

2. *The Marne Valley*

This, for tourist purposes, is signposted the *Circuit Rouge*, the red tour. About Epernay the *grands crus* champagnes are:

Mareuil	Ay	Dizy

And on the right bank of the river are:

Cumières	Verneuil
Hautvillers	Vincelles
Damery	Centeuil
Vaudières	Chatillon-sur-Marne

On the left bank:

Epernay	Festigny
Mardeuil	Troissy
Boursault	Dormans
Leuvrigny	

3. *Côtes des Blancs*

So-called for its white grapes, and signposted the *Green Circuit*. This is an area south of the Marne comprising:

Grands crus vineyards:

Cramant	Oger
Avize	Mesnil-sur-Oger

and lesser *crus*:

Chouilly	Cuis	Granves

Still south of the *Côte des Blancs* and outside the main circuit is a small area where vineyards are planted to black grapes yielding two *premiers crus* wines, Vertus and Bergères-les-Vertus. There are other outlying vineyards within the region of Champagne *Appellation d'Origine,* at Vitry-le-

François, Bar-sur-Aube and Bar-sur-Seine. The last named has a separate *Appellation* to cover the *rosé* wines of Riceys.

So much for the list of Champagne vineyards. The history behind these wines is interesting. And, first, the unique cellars of Reims, Epernay and Ay.

The city of Reims takes its name from the Celtic tribe of the Remi, first enemies of the Romans, later their allies and subjects, united with them to fight off the devastating invasions of German barbarians from the north and northeast, an occupation in which they have been engaged at intervals ever since. The Roman city, however, was originally called Durocortorum. Of the connection between the buildings of this city and the *caves* used by the champagne-makers, Mr. Denis Morris has this interesting note:

'The old Roman caves have a much greater depth than more recent, commercial excavations. The former are the quarries from which the Romans took enormous blocks for use in building, for repairs and ramparts. Being somewhat more cultivated than those who desecrate our modern countryside by inflicting deep wounds on large surfaces, they quarried intelligently, making their excavations in the form of pyramids, which yielded an enormous amount of material without affecting the surface. Standing at the bottom of one of these pyramids, as I did with M. Jean Marc Heidsieck, you can just see a Dutchman's trouser patch of light some 150 feet above. Around you rest hundreds of thousands of bottles of champagne. . . .'[1]

At a higher level are the more modern tunnellings, about 120 miles of them, with more at Epernay and Ay. It is these which provide the space, in correct conditions of temperature and humidity required for the manipulation of 30 million bottles of champagne constantly and slowly passing through them.

The processes undergone by the wine are as follows, and they are described in some detail because there is more to interest the visitor, more action to see, in champagne, than in the case of any other wine excepting those which exactly imitate champagne, such as sparkling Vouvray. Visiting wine-cellars, excepting where tasting is involved, is apt to

[1] *The French Vineyards*. Denis Morris (Eyre and Spottiswoode). An admirable book by one of the rare Englishmen with a first-class wine-palate.

be rather boring after you have seen one or two, but the manipulations of wine are, in the case of champagne, more diverse, for it is not altogether a 'natural' wine.

The pressing is done in hydraulic presses which hold about four metric tons of grapes at a time. As the grapes, excepting from the *Côtes des Blancs*, are black, there is a danger of tinting the wine pink unless the work is done quickly, before any fermentation can start working the pigment out of the skins. On the other hand if at first it is done too brutally, the grading of the juice would be impossible. For whereas relatively gentle, steady pressure extracts juice from the middle, largest cells of the grapes first, free from fragments of pulp, harder pressing smashes the grapes and produces juice of the same mixed quality from the beginning to the end of the pressing. As it is, the work is managed so that the first ten casks of each pressing are the best juice, making the *vin du cuvée*. The rest, produced by much harder pressure sustained for several hours, makes good wine, but it usually has a darker colour and it is not the finest. The holding-off of fermentation, however, is relatively easy because the grapes, and subsequently the standing juice while it is left to clear, are dosed with sulphur dioxide, a gas which sterilizes the *must* and so prevents the yeasts from working. In fact it kills them. It can be applied in several ways: some sulphur salts put into an acid medium in suitable quantity release the sterilizing gas. The method is used by canners in preventing canned fruits and vegetables from fermenting. Or the gas can be fed through the juice from cylinders.

This process, since it kills the yeasts in the juice, entails putting some back when fermentation is required. There are two principal ways of doing this. A sufficient sample of unsterilized juice can be allowed to start fermenting and can then be stirred into the main body of the juice when it is poured into the fermenting vats or casks. The yeasts multiply at a great rate, and there are soon enough of them to deal with whatever quantity of wine is being made. But there is a more scientific way of doing the job, with a great advantage, and it is now very generally practised everywhere in France, although certain vigneron-vintners among the best prefer to avoid using SO_2 and the cultured yeasts about to be described, sticking rigidly to the old ways.

Louis Pasteur discovered, when doing research on the micro-organisms which turn fruit-juice into wine, that not one but many kinds of yeast were involved. The species of yeasts vary from variety to variety and from region to region. They are probably numerous beyond counting. But even on any particular variety of grapes, in any particular region, there are more than one species. Pasteur also discovered that yeasts vary in their 'efficiency' as alcohol producers. The best yeast on any given bunch of grapes—for they are present on the skins of all fruit, in the 'bloom'— can produce, for example, say 10° of alcohol from a sugar content of 20 per cent. Other yeasts also present produce much less with the same amount of raw material. If, therefore, a *must* is allowed to ferment without interference, all the yeasts present will begin to increase and multiply, they will all attack the supply of sugar in their environment, and so not all of that sugar will fall to the most efficient yeasts; some of it will be consumed by inferior strains of yeast, so that the final alcohol content of the wine will be less than it would have been if the most efficient yeast only were present and had all the available sugar to itself.

The modern practice, therefore, is to isolate the best yeast—local strains of 'Pasteur's Yeast' as it is called—and grow a culture of it pure. Then to sterilize the grape juice with sulphur dioxide, thus killing not only the good yeasts but all the yeasts present and, incidentally, any undesirable micro-organisms such as the vinegar bacillus—and to start again by putting a culture of the yeast you want into the sterilized juice once the gas, which is volatile, has passed away, leaving the juice unspoilt. There are now yeasts native to every great wine available in pure culture to all wine-makers from their co-operative laboratories or research stations. Incidentally these same yeasts, being more efficient than apple-yeasts, are now used at Long Ashton Research Station in the making of fine ciders. I repeat that all this is not essential: it is still perfectly possible, and probably better, to make wine as it has been made for thousands of years, that is by letting the fermentation take place of its own accord and without interference. That is how I make my own wine, but then I do not have to produce a standard product for sale, but simply something pleasant and interesting to drink.

Whoever has never helped to work a wine-press, whether manual or hydraulic, would have difficulty in believing the resistance offered by so soft a fruit as the grape to the colossal pressures involved. In the case of red wines and less delicate white wines also, the grapes are *foulés*, trodden, before they are pressed. Nowadays, excepting in remote parts of Italy and Greece, they are not literally trodden, as they used to be, with the feet. The job is done by a simple smashing-machine—as a matter of fact it can be done with an old-fashioned mangle—and what that delivers to the press is a mush of smashed grapes from which it is easy to press the juice. But where delicate white wines are being made and only the juice is wanted, there is no preliminary *foulage*.

Long after it seems that every drop of juice must have been forced out of the grapes, and the remaining hard cake of *marc*, composed of skins and pips, must be as dry as a bone, more juice will trickle out if the *marc* be broken up and pressed again. Hydraulic presses are more efficient than even big manual presses driven from a loft over the body of the press, and very little if any juice is left in the *marc* after the final pressing. It is for this reason that the champagne-makers use only the first pressings for the best wine, a rule followed in the other great vineyards also; and it is for this reason, too, that at least one considerable vigneron-vintner of my acquaintance (no names, no pack-drill), while using hydraulic presses for the wine he *sells*, sticks to an ancient hand press for the wine he drinks! It is probable, as a matter of interest, that from the point of view of purity, clarity, quality, the best 'press' ever used in wine-making was the ancient Egyptian one, which was not a press at all but a gigantic 'tammy cloth' familiar to cooks and housewives. The grapes were trodden by four men who marched round and round in the great tubs, steadying themselves by ropes hung from the roof of the winery, and stamping to the rhythm of music. The trodden pulp—and the human foot never breaks up pips or pulverizes skins—was put into a huge linen cloth which was then folded over it, and four more men, by the aid of long poles tied to the folded ends of this cloth, *wrung* the juice out of the pulp. This would have expressed the free juice without crushing the cells of the grapes, and of course the juice would have been filtered clear of solid particles by having to pass through the linen.

In Champagne the pressing and first fermentation, the *cuvage* of the wine, is usually done by the grower himself. The great Champagne firms with world-famous names buy the young wine from the small growers, and put it through the remainder of the necessary processes themselves. Some of them, of course, also own and work their own vineyards, and it is these which constitute the large holdings in the region. The new wine is still, *champagne naturelle*; and in my heretical opinion it is, after a year or two in bottle, better so than when it is the expensive finished product!

The juice having been allowed to clear and being ready for the fermenting vat, we come to what some English wine-snobs regard as a shameful secret never to be mentioned, but is taken for granted by the French although we do not hear of it in their wine-and-tourist propaganda, perhaps because it suggests that the amount of sunshine enjoyed by France is not quite so generous as we imagine. (It is instructive in this connection, and amusing in view of our own cherished myth about the awfulness of the English climate, to have a look at the official statistics.) This next and unmentionable process is *chaptelisation*, which, as already explained, means adding sugar to the *must*.

I am often asked, concerning the wine of our small vineyard in Kent, 'I suppose you have to add sugar to the juice?' And this question is usually put on a note of tolerant contempt, as if to imply that because of this shocking practice, made necessary by our dreadful summer weather, our Kentish wine is not *really* wine at all. The answer, of course, is that in the ten years we have been making wine we have twice had no vintage at all, and only once been able to avoid *chaptelisation*. And in this respect we differ from the vintners of Champagne, not to mention parts of Alsace, the German Rhine, Lorraine, Luxemburg and Belgium, only in a matter of degree: that is, total failures are one in those countries to two in ours, and sugaring the *must* probably becomes necessary in one year out of three, taking a mean figure over a longish period. The object of this addition of pure cane sugar to the *must* is to give it a sugar content such that the wine produced will have an alcohol content of at least 10°; or to raise the ultimate alcohol content to, say, 12°, the figure depending upon the character of the wine in question.

It might be supposed that since this practice is allowed, and very properly allowed, by law—for the wine thus made is still excellent—there would be no such thing as a total failure. But there are two reasons for such failures, more frequent in Champagne than in any other great viticultural region. And one of them afflicts the Champagne growers, but not ourselves in Kent. That is, spring frosts. In our ten years we have never had a vine damaged in the young leaf and flower-bud by May frosts. Whereas in Champagne this very frequently happens, and in bad years the entire crop may be wiped out by a single cold night before the flowers have even had a chance to open. What happens is that the young spring shoots of the vines, bearing the flower-buds still enclosed, are scorched by frost and simply wither the following day. The vines 'shoot' again, of course, but in the case of *V. vinifera* varieties this second production of shoots is unfruitful. In the case of most *hybrid* varieties, the second crop of shoots *is* fruitful, so that, even after a severe and disastrous frost, the grower of hybrids usually gets from half to three-quarters of a normal crop. But in Champagne we are in a region of *Appellation Contrôllée* and no hybrid vines may be planted. The second reason for total failure is the one we in England suffer from more, not less, often than do the Champagne growers, and that is persistently cool and wet summers or very cold springs which, even without frost, so delay the vines that the grapes come too late to ripen properly. Now, *chaptelisation* cannot be used with positively unripe grapes. It can be used only where the grapes are ripe but their sugar content inadequate for want of sun. If they are positively unripe, then not only will the sugar content of the juice be inadequate, but the acidity of the juice will be so high that the wine would taste horribly acid. No amount of sugar added will correct this fault. There are, it is true, other ways of dealing with it: it is possible to add water to the *must* so that the final proportion of acid to the whole is correct—wine must be acid or it will have neither character nor bouquet; it is also possible to lower the acidity of wine by adding an alkali to the *must*, or even to the finished wine. The one which is used by English vintners and by others outside the control of the wine laws, is chalk. It was of this practice that Sir John Falstaff is complaining in the famous reproach,

'You rogue, there's lime in this sack!'

Neither of these practices is legal in the principal French vineyards, and the second, certainly, is pernicious, for it ruins the character of wine and gives it an insipid flatness. Consequently, in the years when grapes do not ripen enough to come within the limits of tolerable acidity, there is nothing whatever to be done, and there is no vintage.

So much for the sugaring of the *must*.

Champagnes are made from blended wines, that is from the wines of different vineyards, and the variation in qualities as between one *grand cru* or *premier cru* and another is in some measure due to this blending. There is another aspect of blending: the great houses with a reputation to lose and a commercial need to offer a more or less standard product, hold back some wine of the best years to blend it with the wine of lesser years, so that buyers can pretty well rely on getting a wine of known and recognizable qualities under any given label.

All the above processes are commonplaces of any wine-growing region, but thereafter the special champagne techniques come into it.

The wine is bottled in the spring following the vintage, and then taken down into the chalk or rock *caves* already described. This is done just before the second fermentation begins, so that it takes place in the bottle. Now fermenting liquors throw off a scum, a deposit of lees consisting of an agglomeration of small solid particles, dead and living yeasts and precipitates of acids, mainly tartaric acid. They also give off a large amount of gas, CO_2, a by-product of the yeasts' work in turning sugar into alcohol. It is this gas which produces the pressure inside a champagne bottle, that is, which make the wine sparkling. It is likewise this gas which makes champagne so elevating to the spirits, for it carries volatile alcohol 'to the head', as they say, very quickly. The major skill in champagne-making consists in the task of ridding each bottle of the deposit of lees, without losing the pressure, or for that matter the wine! The process in question is called *dégorgement*, and we will come to it after a short discursion into history.

Champagne invented itself: second ferments occurring in the bottle, and the subsequent drinking, in curiosity or despair, of the wine by the grower, revealed that the process was not a disaster, but a godsend. However, all was not roses, for the bottles of the time were not strong enough, nor were they so shaped, as to stand the pressure inside them. Nor was 'corking' with oiled-rag bungs, a process then common, so effective as to hold the genie of the champagne firmly imprisoned. The wine was for ever blowing its top; or, if you did stop the bottle with wood or cork wired on, then the bottles burst. The losses, in the early days of champagne-making, due to this bursting, were fantastic: up to 50 per cent of the vintage. And, incidentally, the danger to the cellarers was considerable. Nor has this difficulty been entirely overcome. The losses due to bursting are no longer very serious, but it is impossible to spend very long in one of the underground tunnels of Reims or Epernay without hearing the bang of an exploding bottle.

The man who made champagne a manageable wine for commerce was the Brother Cellarer of the Abbey of Haut-villers in the second half of the eighteenth century. His name was Perignon. Although Dom Perignon has never been so much as beatified, let alone canonized, by the Pope, in Champagne he has the status of a patron saint and folk hero. His life work on the wines of Champagne lasted nearly half a century. Reading the Abbé Monceaux's account of the Abbey, which contains a biography of Dom Perignon as vintner, it becomes clear that this monk was what we would now call a man of science. His rational approach, his infinite patience in trial-and-error methods, his intellectual integrity, were all typical of the best and rarest kind of scientist. His achievements were to make the judgement of the state of ripeness in the grapes a matter of near-certainty; to make blending rational instead of hit-and-miss; and to go some way towards bringing the destructive demon of pressure in the bottles under some sort of control. In short, although handicapped by want of instruments and forced to rely on his senses instead, he laid down the basic techniques for champagne-making which are still viable. Nowadays the growers rely on a form of spectrometer to ascertain the sugar content of their grapes, instead of the palate. But whereas the instrument is perfectly accurate as to sugar, it is silent in the matter of other qualities, and it is very possible that the palate and nose of Dom Perignon, or for that matter of the usually elderly workers who are often the most valuable men about any wine-making undertaking, are subtler instruments more apt to make the wine excellent than any such tool as we have mentioned.

The deep cellars of the Champagne towns are equipped with special racks called *pupitres*, and in these the bottles are laid. Remember that there are tens of millions involved every year. Every day each bottle is given a twist, a shake, and a slight tilt downwards, so that the bottles point with their corks ever more sharply towards the ground. The twist, shake and tip are such as to keep the lees, produced by second ferment in the bottle, on the move towards the cork. The end of this process finds the bottle standing upside-down with all the deposit—mostly tartar—lying on the inside end of the cork.

Dégorgement, the next process, is highly skilled work. The *dégorgeur* holds the bottle pointing at an angle just below the horizontal and works out the cork with his fingers until the pressure in the bottle blows the cork and the sediment with it, out, when the bottle is sharply uprighted to minimize the loss of wine. The final process consists in topping up the bottles to make good the loss, and recorking, both of which have to be done swiftly.

Champagne at this stage is so dry that it is almost un-drinkable by most people, although those who are accustomed to drink wines made in cold countries often like it.

(It is significant that white wine made in England from one of the tiny vineyards of white grapes which have come into existence in the last ten years, makes surprisingly good sparkling wine. In the same connection, here is a quotation from the Hon. Charles Hamilton's account of his eighteenth-century wine-making enterprise at Pains Hill. The vineyard in question was planted on the south slope of a gentle hill, the soil being sand and gravel. Hamilton says: 'It is planted entirely with two sorts of Burgundy grapes, the Auvernat[1], which is the most delicate but the tenderest, and the Miller grape,[2] commonly called the Black Cluster, which is most hardy.' The first year red wine was made but was a failure, the wine being 'so very harsh and austere that I despaired of ever making red wine fit to drink'. Hamilton then tried white wine, by pressing his grapes without treading them first. 'That experiment succeeded far beyond my most sanguine expectations, for the very first year I made white wine it nearly resembled the flavour of champagne.'

In subsequent years Hamilton made 'champagne' which, as he says, 'sparkled and creamed in the glass'. His method of making it, however, was extraordinary: the wine was fermented in sealed vats of wood held from bursting by powerful reinforcements of beams and battens. Even so, such was the pressure that the wine oozed through the very wood of the casks. Heaven knows how the bottling was done; it must have entailed bathing in a fountain of sparkling wine. Hamilton's conclusion is amusing in the light of my own experience as a vintner. 'Such is the prejudice of most people against anything of English growth I generally found it most prudent not to declare where it grew until they had passed their verdict upon it.' A similar precaution enabled me to pass off some of our home-grown Riesling-Sylvaner as a fair hock.[3]

To return to the excessive dryness of new champagne.

[1] Pinot Noir.   [2] Pinot Meunier.
[3] The quotations in this parenthesis are taken from William Speechley's *Treatise on the Vine or Grape-tree* (York, 1780). This admirable book by the greatest head-gardener and grape-breeder of his day, also contains numerous accounts of other English vineyards, although not, of course, the Marquis of Bute's Glamorganshire one, which was a century later.

To deal with this, advantage is taken of the topping-up process to add sweetness to the wine. Even for the *brut* wines, the extra-dry preferred in England, a small fraction of the wine added is actually a syrup of cane sugar. And this fraction is increased in accordance with the final rating of the wine: for sweet champagne it may be as much as 15 per cent, less for *demi-sec*, *sec*, etc. Thus there is no difference between a *brut* champagne and a sweet champagne, excepting that artificially produced by the addition of sugar-syrup.

The law requires the champagne-makers to keep their wine in cellar for one more year after this process, after which it can be released for sale. But in the case of the better wines it may be kept much longer, up to five years. And as in the case of other fine wines, champagne has its 'vintage' years. These tend to run in series, demonstrating that weather cycles are more than one year long; or to be rare. Thus between 1864 and 1874 there were only two very good years. On the other hand the wines of 1889, 1893 and 1895 were all outstanding.

It is difficult for me to arrive at the facts as to whether a champagne of a really great year can be drunk with pleasure at a great age. Some champagne lovers hold that the wine can and should be drunk old; others that fifteen years is the limit. Old champagne is hard to come by, but if you have enough money in your pocket while you are there, you had better make trial of this matter for yourself.

Some quite pleasant red wines are made in the region for local consumption, but in my opinion the wine for the visitor to drink while in the country is 'still' champagne. The more famous sparkling wine can be bought anywhere in the world, and not much if at all dearer than in Reims. Whereas, for most people, still champagnes are a novelty. These wines, if produced within the geographical and viticultural limits laid down under the *Appellation d'Origine* rules, are entitled to call themselves *vins naturels de Champagne,* and they have, at their best, all the light, subtle, aromatic delicacy of the most northerly wines. Those who, like myself, find that whatever they may do for one's

party spirit, bubbles paralyse the palate, can by seeking and
drinking natural champagne discover the tastes which
underlie that golden, bursting exuberance which Dom
Perignon left, perhaps one of the most valuable legacies any
people has ever received, to his fellow countrymen.

Note on dégorgement

In the case of some sparkling wines the process has been
facilitated by a modern invention; the wine nearest the cork,
and which holds the lees, is briefly and locally frozen solid.
This minimises losses of both wine and pressure.

CHAPTER SIX

THE WINES OF ALSACE AND LORRAINE...

O R, rather, of Lorraine and Alsace, for that is the lie of the land in the direction we are moving. You take the road from Reims to St. Menhould, which stands near to the edge of the great plain of Champagne. A few miles to the east of that town, on the road to Verdun, the land begins to climb. At Verdun you cross the Meuse and make for Metz; there you are on the Moselle. And although the French regard the vineyards of that river as of very secondary importance, they are historically interesting, 'touristically' attractive, and oenologically worth visiting if only because the pale, clean wines of the Moselle should be known, and compared with those farther north on the same river, the obscure wines of Luxemburg and the great wines of Germany. For there are vineyards at intervals all along the course of that lovely river in its narrow valley between high mountains until, at Koblenz, they join hands with those of the Rhine.

Although Moselle wines are both oenologically and commercially less important than those of Alsace, they have the more ancient lineage. Whereas everything concerning the origins of the Alsatian vineyards is speculation, we have written evidence that the wines of Lorraine were already established and reputed in the fourth century. The great vineyard of the Moselle valley described by Ausonius was clearly of commercial importance. This Latin poet was a Frenchman, for he was born at Bordeaux, so that he certainly knew a good deal about vineyards and wine. He became a barrister and had a very distinguished career, being appointed tutor to Gratian, the son of the emperor Valentinian. When Gratian became emperor he made his old teacher prefect of three provinces, including Gaul, and Consul in the year 379. And the most valuable of his surviving writings is his *Mosella*, about the river of that name. Ausonius died in 388. His consulship, and the date of his death, enable us to date his work within a decade or so, hence our ability to say that the Moselle vineyards were established and by no means new in the middle of the fourth century. Nor, probably, were they very old. For they must have been planted after Domitian's decree against viticulture in the provinces had been reversed by Probus in 280.

Moselle, Alsace and Jura wines are all grown and made in country far more attractive to the visitor than Champagne or Burgundy. There are no doubt people who do prefer great plain vistas to river-and-mountain country, but most people will find the constantly changing scene of Lorraine, the steep climbs and descents, the narrow valleys and worked hillsides, much more agreeable. Moreover, this eastern, Franco-German world is much less familiar; its quaint—it is the only word—villages, the extreme peasantry of its peasants, its bells, its mountain flocks, its storks and its unfamiliar food, all have the charm of novelty.

Lorraine produces both VDQS[1] wines, and *vin courant*, the ordinary, nameless wine drunk by the people every day with their meals.

By far the best way to become familiar with these ordinary wines, as with the admirable *charcuterie* of the provinces, both in Lorraine and elsewhere in France, is to make your midday meal a picnic. You can then eat dinner at your inn at night, and with it try the VDQS and *grands crus* wines. Carry a good large straw- or wicker-covered bottle of some kind—if you are ever in Tuscany the most beautiful ones can be bought for a few shillings at any village shop—and whenever it is empty have it filled from the wood at the nearest *débit de vin*. And keep a note, if only a mental note,

[1] VDQS, i.e. *Vins de qualité supérieur*. This descriptive phrase, *wine of superior quality*, is not just arbitrary, but defines wines of a specific quality and produced in specific ways from certain grapes, under the *Appellation d'Origine* rules. It is commonly shortened to VDQS and appears thus on wine labels.

of what you drink and how you like it. From time to time you will get something nasty, but that is in the nature of learning by experience, and in compensation you will sometimes get something surprisingly good for very little to pay, always an agreeable experience. In Lorraine you are fairly safe, for the ordinary wines are made from the same grapes as the VDQS wines in most places, although harvested from the less-favoured slopes.

But there is another reason to make a point of this practice in Lorraine: in some parts of the Moselle, as in some parts of the Meuse, valleys, there are plantations of the much-feared hybrid vines mentioned in Chapter I. The principal varieties planted are not the latest, and as the more recently bred *cépages* are improvements on the older hybrids, the wine is not the best that can be made from such grapes. Nevertheless there are vineyards of certain good ones, Seibel 54.55, Oberlin 545 and Baco 1, the latter a variety which has proved itself very useful to us in east Kent. There may also be some of the newer and better hybrids under field trial. Such vines, and also, by the way, the wines made from their grapes, are sometimes referred to by the initials PD, and you should be warned that these initials were until recently, and in some circles still are, a term of abuse, whether applied to wine or to dessert grapes. In wine they imply the famous *gout de fox* of Canadian wine, and in grapes the sliminess of texture and the unpleasant taste of liquorice which some people like in such table varieties as the Strawberry grape and the Framboise grape. The word *fox* in *gout de fox* does not apply to the animal, but refers either to the name of the rank-flavoured American wild grape called the Fox grape (*V. vulpina*) a flavour also present in the *V. labrusca* much used by early breeders of American × Old World varieties; or it refers to a Mr. Fox, who was apparently an American vine-breeder of the nineteenth century. Nobody seems to know which is the real derivation of the word.

These initials PD stand for *Producteur Direct*, in reference to the fact that the hybrid varieties in question were not simply root-stocks which had to be grafted with French scions before they would produce good grapes, which was the first use of hybrids; but varieties bearing their own crop of wine or dessert grapes. Very, very slowly the initials are losing their pejorative quality as more and more hybrids are bred free from the taint of *V. labrusca* and other 'foxy' species.

Most of these new wines from hybrid grapes are ordinary wines, bottled or from the wood, and, if bottled, bearing little more on the label than a figure stating their content of alcohol, which has to be there because it governs the price. But it is sometimes possible, by falling into friendly talk with an innkeeper, to discover a local enthusiast for one or several of the new *cépages*. He will usually be a member of a nation-wide organization called FENAVINO (*Fédération Nationale d'Etudes et de Défence des Nouveaux Cépages Français issue de l'hybridation et de métissage*. Those knowing French will wonder about the apparent tautology in this mouthful: by general agreement an arbitrary decision was made to confine the term 'hybrid' to the offspring of different *species*; *métis* vines, by the same arbitrary arrangement, are crosses between *V. vinifera* varieties. Thus all hybrids, as the word is used in grape-breeding, have American blood, e.g. all the 'new' vines of Seyve-Villard, Bertille Seyve, Baco, Landot, Ravat, Tissier-Ravat, Pirovano, Ubizzoni, and others. *Métis* vines have no American in their breeding; they are, e.g. Riesling × Sylvaner, Madeleine × Sylvaner, etc.).

If you can contrive to meet such a man and lead him to propose a wine-tasting, do so. His PD wines will be more carefully vinted than most, he will have kept some good wine to age, tried his hand at blending. Only if as many unbiased strangers as possible, with no shares in the copper or sulphur industries and no interest vested in a plantation of PD vines, taste and judge the new wines, will they be given the chance which the authorities are trying to take from them—to prove themselves.

As to the food to eat for your picnic, it is usually wise to concentrate on the local bread, butter, cheeses, *charcuterie* and fruit. Never picnic out of tins; you can always do that in such benighted countries as have no fresh food, and France is not, thank God, of their number.

Then as to your dinner wine: Lorraine has no *grands vins*, but its VDQS are excellent, delicate, dry, pale wines, some almost green, superlatively refreshing on hot days, good to drink with meals or courses of fish, or for that matter to drink between meals. The two principal Moselle groups are:

Côtes de Toul

These come from the wine-growing *communes* to the west and south-west of Toul in the Meurthe-et-Moselle *département*. The most important *cépage* planted is a variety of the great Gamay family called *Gamay de Toul*, or sometimes *Gamay de Liverdun*. This produces a pale, off-gold wine locally known as *vin gris*—the *grey wine* for which Toul is famous among wine connoisseurs, and which tastes and is much better than its rather dismal name would seem to imply.

Côtes de Moselle

These wines are all from within the Moselle *département*, where the *encépagement*—the collection of varieties grown— is more diverse than in Meurthe-et-Moselle. For *Appellation d'Origine* purposes, however, it is limited to Gamay, Pinot and three we now encounter for the first time, *Sylvaner, Riesling* and *Traminer*. As they are essentially Alsace varieties, or Rhine varieties, it will be as well to describe them and their performance in that country. I have personal preference for the green Sylvaner grown in Moselle over its relative of the Rhine; it is one of the most fragrant and beautifully coloured of wines, and I know no better specific against a heatwave.

*　*　*　*　*　*

The short way from the wines of Lorraine to the wines of Alsace, from Moselle to Rhine, is from Metz via Château Salins, to Strasbourg. On the other hand, if you have no objection to crossing frontiers, Trier, known for its wines since the fourth century, is well worth a visit, and there comparison can be made between the Moselle wines of France and those of Germany. From Trier you turn south-west, climb mountains to something over 3,000 feet, and drop down to Neunkirchen, thence to Saarbruken and over a fast road to Strasbourg, which is the urban heart of the great Alsatian valley, and the centre of the wine district in which we are now interested, a valley about twenty miles wide between its mountains, extending from about Lauterburg on the Rhine in the north, to Colmar on the Rhine in the south.

At first sight it may seem singular that the people who, late in the third or early in the fourth century, could see and exploit the possibilities for viticulture in the narrow valley of the Moselle, should have neglected the far more favourable conditions on the Rhine, farther east, which is nevertheless what happened if it be true that the Moselle vineyards are of older establishment than the Alsatian. But as a matter of fact there was an economically important reason for this. The importance of rivers as a means of freight-carrying in the third and fourth centuries cannot be exaggerated. It is probably true to say that there was simply no point in establishing a commercial vineyard at a point where there was no navigable river to make exporting the wine, if only into the next province, fairly easy. Now the river Moselle, considering only the reaches here in question, offered no exceptional difficulties or dangers to the Gallo-Roman boatmen or lightermen. But although the Rhine farther north, from the point where Lauterburg grew up as a riparian port, was possible for freight-carrying boats, the nature of that river, up to and for centuries after the epoch in question, all the way up the Alsatian plain from Colmar to Lauterburg, was such as to make it very difficult and dangerous not only for boats and lighters but even for settlements, since flooding was apt to wipe out whole villages. These reaches of the river were, until in 1870 the work of clearing and embanking a main channel was undertaken, very shallow and fast. They constantly broke up into very numerous side arms and backwaters and alternative courses. The water poured over stone and gravel beds, falling 50 inches per mile, so that in places the current was torrential and the boatmen had virtually to negotiate rapids which were for ever changing their course. The river here was in fact so useless to the inhabitants that they turned their backs on it and built their villages, including the first town of Strasbourg, on the more tranquil river Ill. At all events the Rhine offered the Alsatians no outlet for wine, and consequently they did not plant vines. And that this want of an outlet really was the reason is probably shown by the fact that, north of Lauterburg, where the river became navigable, there are archaeological remains of an ancient viticultural industry. Moreover, as Professor Roger Dion has pointed out in this connection,[1] the most ancient Roman settlements on the river are also north of Lauterburg, e.g. Germersheim (*Vicus Julii*) and Worms (*Vangiones*).

As for written evidence, there is nothing about an Alsatian wine industry until Carolingian times—the eighth and early ninth centuries. But since the river between Colmar and Lauterburg was not tamed until 1870, how is it that what was impossible in the fourth century became possible in the eighth or a little earlier? Professor Dion again suggests an answer: there was an advance in lightering techniques. The Frisians, anxious to trade their beautifully dyed woollen cloths for Alsatian wines—presumably a certain number of small vineyards had made these known—mastered the river by means of lightweight, manageable *barques,* and their skill as river navigators. And this would have given the necessary stimulus to wider planting of the vine in Alsace. There is another possibility which Professor Dion does not consider: that the river itself may have grown tamer in the course of three centuries.

The vineyards of Alsace are in two groups, those of the Haut Rhin *département* and those of the Bas Rhin. They cling to the east and south-east faces of the Vosges, the lowest being more than 650 feet above sea-level, the highest not much less than 1,400 feet. Thus they command the narrow Alsatian plain from Thann, south of Colmar, to Marlenheim, north-west of Strasbourg.

As in Champagne there is a *route du vin,* a wine-road, but in this case it is a nice straight line. Drive out from Strasbourg to Marlenheim, turn south, and you can drive down through the whole picturesque string of wine villages which, from north to south, are as follows:

[1] *Nouvelle Revue Française,* Feb. 1, 1954.

Wangen	Kientzheim
Obernai	Ammerschwihr
Gertwiller	Turckheim
Barr	Wintzenheim
Mittelbergheim	Wettolsheim
Bergheim	Eguisheim
Ribeauville	Husseren-les-châteaux
Hunawihr	Voegtlinschoffen
Zellenberg	Bollenberg
Riquewihr	Westhalten
Mittelwihr	Orschwihr
Sigolsheim	Guebwiller . . .

and probably some others.

These villages have what is called a 'continental' climate: their winters are very cold and snowbound, but then the vine is extremely winter-hardy. Their summers are correspondingly warm, which is what matters. And their combined mean annual rain-cum-snow fall is adequate, though only just, being about 23 inches a year. As to the soils of these village vineyards, they are very diverse: there are very ancient strata side by side with quarternary volcanic, and even chalk subsoils. All, however, are more or less favourable to the vine.

From the visitor's point of view the Alsatian wine country is equal in charm—although very different, of course—to the Dordogne. The well-wooded and constantly changing mountain vistas, streams, belled mountain sheep, wooden houses, châlet-styles, ancient and curious churches —it is a sort of Switzerland but with far more character than that picture-postcard country. Its charms are perhaps of the more obvious kind, but they are none the worse for that. Hotel accommodation, in agreeable, small inns, not international caravanserai, is pleasant, clean and, by modern standards, cheap. The food is very good indeed, interestingly different from that of other parts of France and copious in quantity. And the wines, of course, superb. Riquewihr, in the Bas-Rhin, with hardly a building later than 1550, a thirteenth-century belfry, and flower-grown fortress walls, is as pleasant a town as any I know.

There are two kinds of viticulture practised: smallholding, which accounts for most of the acreage under vines, and big 'domaines' exploited by large firms. There are approximately 24,000 acres of vineyards in the two départements, and these are owned and cultivated by no fewer than 50,000 proprietor-viticulteurs. This means that, since a few big firms have as much as 250 acres each, some of the small-holdings are of the order of a quarter of an acre. But at an average planting density of 3,200 vines to the acre, even so tiny a holding will have about 800 vines to be cared for.

Roughly speaking, a quarter-acre holding of this kind, worked by a man in his spare time—yet not as a mere hobby for he will be highly skilled, altogether professional—has an annual output of 160 gallons of wine, equivalent to nearly 1,000 bottles. It is extremely difficult to get at reliable figures, but this might probably represent an annual return, after the owner's time and materials have been paid for at standard rates, of something like £75 per annum, a high figure for a quarter of an acre. The whole Alsatian wine industry produces about 17 million gallons of wine annually, but by no means all of this output is entitled to the Appellation vin d' Alsace which here, as elsewhere, depends on site, methods of pruning and cultivation, and above all on the cépages planted. Rather more than half the annual production is, by these rules, vin d'Alsace.

The cépages in question are:

For white wines of VDQS standard and above	Traminer Riesling Pinot Muscat Sylvaner
For other white wines	Chasselas Knipperlé Goldriesling Burger (syn. Ebling)

The name Muscat is misleading, for there are scores of muscat varieties, of all sizes and seasons from the extremely early small-berried, shy-cropping Perle de Czaba to the superb great Muscat of Alexandria of our hothouses. The

Muscat of Alsace is a local variety with the distinctive muscat flavour. Chasselas is familiar to English gardeners under the misnomer *Royal Muscadine*, a grape which is neither a muscat nor a muscadine (muscadines are American wild grapes of species classified under the sub-genus *Muscadinia*, or ought to be), and which ripens well on walls here. It is much grown in Switzerland for wine, and in France, notably about Paris, for table grapes, though it is slowly giving way way to some of the best hybrid half-muscats which are as early, larger and better flavoured.

For red wines { Pinot Noir (*syn.* Burgunder)
{ Other Pinots, notably Meunier.

The grapes of these vines are harvested very late, sometimes even in early November. The date for this vintage is not an arbitrary one, at the discretion of the individual proprietor of the vineyard. He, at the risk of losing his status as a grower of *Appellation Controllée* wine, must wait until the Committee of Regional Experts announces the date for the vintage, the Committee members being experts appointed by the Minister of Agriculture advised by his technicians. This same august body announces, at the same time, whether *chaptelisation*, sugaring of the *must*, will be necessary and permitted that year, and to what extent.

Alsace is exceptional in its method of naming wines. Elsewhere, as we have seen, wine-names are usually place-names, villages, parishes, châteaux and so forth. In Alsace the wines are, as a rule, named after the variety of vine from which they derive.

Sylvaner is, in Alsace, a sort of dual-purpose vine, in that it yields either a *grand vin* sold in bottles with an *Appellation Controllée* label or an ordinary wine drawn from the wood and served at table in a pitcher. The ultimate use of the wine depends in this case on the site of the vineyard, not on the variety. Here as on the Moselle, Sylvaner is a green-gold wine, acid, fragrant and refreshing. We tried the vine in Kent for five years, but although fruitful, its grapes never came near ripening, and there can be no doubt that in this sense it is an 'unsuitable' *cépage* for so northerly a vineyard as Alsace, of which more anon.

Chasselas, which ripens easily in southern England on a wall, and in good years also ripens in the open unprotected, is replacing the ancient and shy-cropping varieties Gold-riesling, Knipperlé and Burger. This is a pity: a hundred years ago Dr. Jules Guyot condemned the wine of Chasselas as 'detestable'; it is certainly not very distinguished. However, small vineyards of these are still in cultivation and their wines are to be had from the wood. Incidentally, wine served to you at a meal, in a pitcher, under the name of *zwicker*, is a blend of one or more varieties.

The typical *grand vin cépage* of Alsace is Riesling, a vine so late and slow to ripen its fruit in cold climates (though it behaves very differently in the warmer ones, such as the mountains of Chili where it has been remarkably success-ful), that it cannot be relied upon to ripen on a south wall in Kent without a glass cover. It is a vigorous and fruitful plant, the small bunches of small grapes being a luminescent amber when ripe.

The enquiring novice will be inclined to wonder why, with scores of earlier, faster-ripening varieties to choose from, the Alsatians persist in growing Riesling and Sylvaner, both relatively difficult *cépages* in their climate, so that both varieties require the best, fully exposed sites, yield their harvest late, and too often require *chaptelisation*. The answer is perhaps one of the finest tributes which one can pay to the preoccupation of the French *viticulteurs* with quality. Ries-ling, and to a lesser extent Sylvaner, yield fine and delicate wines having certain specific qualities: they have a charac-teristic colour, bouquet, alcohol content, a high but not excessive acidity. When you put down your money for a bottle of *grand vin d'Alsace*, it is these qualities which you expect to receive in return for it. The Alsatians could, with less trouble to themselves and supposing that the law allowed them to do so, plant any one of half a dozen varieties I could name offhand which would give them less trouble and a larger vintage of perfectly adequate quality. But the wine would not be what has come to be expected of Alsace; so perhaps it is not so much virtue as interest which is vested in these difficult *cépages*.

Traminer: the Traminer vine yields what I take to be the

best of all Alsatian wines, bottled under that name. It is at the same time dry and full-bodied, it has none of the thin curtness of Riesling, and its marked fruitiness gives it a particular distinction. It is for these reasons that it is cultivated with loving care, for although easier to ripen and indeed rather earlier than Riesling, it is a very poor cropper indeed. It was one of the vines which, in our early days, we tried in Kent, and had it not been so hard to crop, it would have solved all our difficulties, for we found that its tiny, pearly grapes, pale gold, opalescent, and shot with a strange mauve light, ripened very well indeed in our open vineyard. But we could not induce it to bear anything like a real crop. Every known and several invented ways of pruning it were tried, but the vines would not carry more than an occasional bunch of grapes. So good are these, however, that we are still trying, this time on the harsh and stony soil of an ancient, ploughed-up road. Difficulties of the same order but in a much lesser degree afflict the skilled growers of Alsace, but because of the quality of the wine which Traminer yields them, they continue to wrestle with them.

There is, by the way, a selected strain of Traminer even better than the parent variety, which is called *Gewurtztraminer* or *Savagnin Rose aromatique*, and this yields a superior wine, one of the really great wines of the world at its best. However, it appears that the name *Gewurtztraminer* on a bottle label does not necessarily, or perhaps even usually, mean that the wine was made from grapes of this strain. According to Denis Morris, in the book already quoted, *Gewurtztraminer* wine is made as a rule from selected pickings of the best Traminer grapes (possibly improved by an attack of *pourriture noble?*) and not from the grapes of *Savagnin Rose aromatique*.

Other varieties grown are Pinot, locally called *Clevner*, a white Pinot locally called *Weiss-Clevner*, and, more important than these, a Pinot *gris* which the Alsatians call *Grau-Clevner*, or magnificently, *Tokayer,* which yields a full, smooth, opulent, yet sufficiently acid wine of outstanding fruity-fragrance. Muscat vines give white wines famous for their bouquet and high flavour. I enjoy this musk flavour in grapes, in pine-flavoured strawberries, in d'Arcy Spice apples, and in the best hot-house melons: but not in wine. Blended wines made from any of these *cépages nobles* are served locally as *edelzwicker*.

Age, apart from the necessary minimum time in bottle, plays little part in the quality of Alsace wines. A great Riesling or Traminer might best be drunk at, say, four or five years of age, and some might keep and even improve longer. But as a rule they can perfectly well be drunk at two, or even one, years old.

Alsace, before we leave it, has one great attraction for bird-lovers. It is the summer home of migrant storks, whose great untidy nests are a curious sight on roofs and towers. There are fewer of these great birds than there used to be— at least this is the case according to the old men of the villages—but they are still to be seen and they are cherished, for they are held to bring luck. It would be a doubly unlucky bird-watcher who did not see a stork at the appropriate time of year somewhere between Colmar and Strasbourg.

CHAPTER SEVEN

BURGUNDY

FROM Colmar make for Mulhouse, thence go through the Belfort Gap and so to the Saône at Vesoul. From there, by way of Langres and Chatillon-sur-Saône, to Chablis. Since the great Burgundy vineyard is divided into several regional vineyards, it will be as well to begin by getting this viticultural geography as clear as possible, referring to the map (pp. 120–121) in order to visualize it.

1. *Basse-Bourgogne*—Lower Burgundy, although, latitudinally speaking, it is 'higher'.

The most important part of this is the Chablis vineyard centred on the town of that name in the *département* of the Yonne. The total area under vines for the production of the *grand vin* entitled to be called Chablis does not exceed a thousand acres, although there is a good deal more planted to vines for subsistence viticulture. The thousand acres are all on the chalk slopes falling towards the river Serein, and they are owned by a large number of smallholders.

Second, and oenologically much less important, about ten thousand acres of the Yonne *département* produce wine entitled to call itself Burgundy. It is sound wine of no distinction and you may be drinking it whenever you buy an otherwise unspecified Burgundy. It need not detain us.

2. *Haute-Bourgogne*—High Burgundy. The *high* and *low* in these denominations refer to altitude, not latitude. Thus High Burgundy is a ridge of highland running north-east to south-west. The most famous wine slopes are those of the Côte d'Or between Dijon in the north and Chagny in the south. The ridge extends, with interruptions, right through the Mâconnais and into Beaujolais, where it broadens into a massif of granitic hills.

That is the north-to-south formation. Considering the same region from east-to-west it comprises (*a*) La Plaine—flat land from the foot of the famous slopes down to the Saône, where ordinary wines are grown and much of which was formerly marsh and is kept dry by an elaborate system of land drainage. (*b*) La Côte—the heart of the great wine country. And (*c*) L'Arrière Côte, which is beyond and higher than La Côte, its altitude varying between about 1,000 and 1,400 feet above sea-level, and producing lesser, although still notable, wines.

3. *Le Mâconnais*—This is in the *département* of Saône-et-Loire. The vineyards of importance are confined to a narrow strip of highlands, part of the same system as the Côte d'Or, on the hills and crests of land west of a line Tournus-Romanèche, between the Saône valley and a line of pleasantly wooded hills.

4. *Beaujolais*—Although this region is considered part of the Burgundy vineyard, the people of Beaujolais insist that their wine is *not* Burgundy but Beaujolais, a different and distinct wine. And there are marked differences, as we shall see.

Lyon may be taken as the southern limit of the Burgundy vineyard. We shall deal with these four regions from north to south in geographical order, but before we come to them something should be said concerning the origin of viticulture in this part of France.

*   *   *   *   *   *

It was long supposed that viticulture as far north as Dijon was of very great antiquity, dating from before the first century of our era. The reason for this supposition was that since, as we have seen, there were vineyards right up to the Rhine by the third century, and since the Burgundy valley, known to geographers as the Rhodanian corridor, is not only farther south but connected with such regions of known pre-Christian wine-growing as the Narbonnaise and the Mediterranean generally, the art and practice of wine-growing and making had used this route to reach the north. It is in fact probable that there were small domestic vineyards as far north as Dijon during the first century, but they were of no importance commercially, although they may well have been very important oenologically as showing what could be done.

There was, moreover, another reason for the mistaken attribution of a prosperous and commercially important viticulture to several regions north of Lyon as early as the year 70, and this is a highly speculative and now discredited reading of a passage in the elder Pliny's *Natural History* (XIV. 18). In this passage Pliny mentions not only a vine variety called Allobrogica, after the tribe which cultivated it and which had already made the wines of Vienne famous, but three other varieties, namely *Taburno, Sotano* and *Ellinco*. For no very good reason these three names were interpreted as corruptions of three other words, to wit, *Arverno, Sequano* and *Helvico*, which just goes to show what happens to scholars who are trying to prove something, instead of trying to find something out. For if these were the real names, then by analogy with the case of the vine *Allobrogica*, their obvious reference to tribal names meant that there were named local *cépages* proper to the Auvergne and to Franche-Comté before the year 70. However, as I have said, the assumption that Pliny's three wine names were corruptions was in any case speculative. And as there is good reason to suppose that there was no wine-growing on the Côte d'Or, let alone the other places involved, for at least another couple of hundred years, it is sounder to adopt the other explanation of these three names, that is that they, like *Allobrogica*, referred to vines and wines grown in the neighbourhood of Vienne.[1]

As to the good reason referred to above, that there was no vineyard on the Côte d'Or until much later than the year 70, there are really two quite separate reasons, one economic and the other technical; and both are of sufficient interest to be touched on here.

The researches of historians have established that the great prosperity of Lyon from the beginning and throughout the century of the Antonnines was due to the predominance in that city's thriving commerce of a great cor-

[1] In this connection see Dion, R., *op. cit.* and also Camille Julian, *Histoire de la Gaule.*

poration of *negotiatores vinarii*, wine merchants whose business was the exporting of wines from the south to the north. This prosperity could simply not have been a fact if, well to the north of Lyon and therefore nearer to the markets, was a flourishing viticulture. And the proof of this is that when at last that flourishing viticulture did come into being further north, the prosperity of the *negotiatores vinarii* of Lyon declined until—the quality of Burgundy wines asserting itself—these gentlemen prospered again by sending northern wines to the south.[1]

As for the technical reason, it has the distinction of having for a long time served on the opposite side of the argument. What it actually shows is that although there was no viticulture on the Côte d'Or during the first, or probably most of the second centuries, it was established in the neighbourhood not much later.

In the year 312 the emperor Constantine paid an official visit to the city of Autun, and it is clear from what transpired in the course of it that the *pagus Arebrignus*, the country now called the *côte de Nuits* and the *côte de Beaune*, was already famous for its wine. But the question is, for how long had it been so? The rhetor, that is the official orator of Autun, in his address to the Roman emperor, said, among much else, this:

'This famous canton, well known for its wine-growing, is very far from deserving the envy with which it is regarded. On the one hand it has its back to a land of mountains and impenetrable forests, where wild beasts have their hidden lairs. On the other hand it overhangs a great flat plain extending to the Saône. True, it is claimed that this plain was formerly flourishing, but that was at a time when the labour of cultivating it was never relaxed, and when every farmer kept his drains free of obstruction, thus clearing the land of water. But nowadays, as a consequence of the devastations, the ditches are obstructed, and these same lowlands which formerly owed their fertility to their situation, are falling back into a state of bog and marsh.

[1] Emile Desjardins, in his *Geographie de la Gaule Romaine* (Vol. 1, p. 448 of the 1876 edition) interpreting inscriptions found at Lyon in this connection, says that the commercial importance of this city in the wine trade was due to its situation '. . . on the northerly limit of the wine-growing lands of the Narbonnaise'.

'As for the vineyards, those vineyards which are so much admired by people ignorant of their real condition, they are so exhausted by age that they hardly respond at all to the care we lavish on them. The vine-stocks, whose age we no longer know, have, by the interlacing of their thousands of roots, formed a solid platform which prevents deep digging between them, so that for want of sufficient soil covering the *provins*[1] are exposed to the rain which drowns them and the sun which burns them. And here we have not the advantage common in Aquitaine and other provinces of being able to find almost anywhere room to plant new vineyards, crowded as we are between unbroken, rocky highlands and low-lying land where frosts are to be feared. . . .'[2, 3]

Now this speech was made with a view to getting the emperor to grant some remission of taxes, which he did, by the way; and consequently we must take the rhetor's picture of the miseries of his country with a pinch of salt. But for us the significant passage is that in which he describes the condition of the vineyards. It would obviously have been impractical to lie about this because the emperor Constantine was no fool and like all governments he was greedy for money; his advisers would certainly have gone to see for themselves whether the vineyards were in the state described by the rhetor.

But we may take it these gentlemen were no more expert in viticulture than were those scholars of our own times who took this description of the Nuits and Beaune vineyards in A.D. 312 as incontrovertible evidence for their great antiquity; and, moreover, accepted the rhetor's version of the consequences which must follow, that is the abandonment of the vineyards as hopeless. As it happens, the condition of these vineyards as described by the orator is good proof that they were not more than a century old, and probably much less. Nor would their age, if that was their condition, really have impaired their cropping power or made the rooting of *provins* impossible to determined *vignerons*. Never mind; the pleas served their purpose, the

---

[1] *Provins*. Tip-layers. A cane of the old vine is curved over and bent down and stuck into the soil where it strikes root and forms a new stock, still connected to the old one.

[2] The rhetor was referring, of course, to spring frosts which destroy the young fruit shoots in May.

[3] This quotation is taken from E. Galletier's *Panégyriques latins*, Vol. 2.

taxes were remitted, which is always a great point gained. But what was the viticultural significance of the rhetor's dismal words?

The condition of the modern Burgundy vineyard gives us no help, because all the vines are grafted and planted relatively wide, and the *provignage* system of propagation was given up when *Phylloxera* made growing vines on their own roots impossible. We must therefore go for our information to the pre-*Phylloxera* vineyards. And the few surviving Burgundian vine-growers who are old enough to have practised viticulture under pre-*Phylloxera* conditions do recognize, in the lamentations uttered by the rhetor of Autun in A.D. 312, a kind of damage which vineyards were exposed to before the appearance of grafting and wide planting. On the other hand their answers to questions put to them in the same connection show clearly both that the rhetor had kissed the Blarney stone, and that his fellow-countrymen were not so very experienced in vine-growing.

How long does it take a vineyard of that kind to get into the state described? The answer furnished by the experienced elders of Burgundian viticulture is, 'much less than a hundred years'. The vineyards of Burgundy were planted in an ancient unit of area which is 4 ares 28 centiares, that is 480 square metres. These were planted at such a density, increased by *provignage* at the rate of 80 or 90 *provins* a year, that after only 50 years each unit would be carrying up to 5,000 *rooted vine-stocks*! much more than enough to form a very solid platform of interlacing roots just below the surface of the soil and to a considerable depth. So that the first conclusion from questioning men who, during the last decades of the nineteenth century, were practising wine-growing in much the same style as the Autunois of the fourth century is that vineyards in the state described to the emperor Constantine need not have been planted before, say, A.D. 260, and might well have been planted later. Now it may well be that Nuits and Beaune were among the places which received a dispensation in the matter of the emperor Domitian's decree against provincial viticulture. On the other hand we have no evidence whatsoever that they were favoured by any such dispensation. And as the decree was

not reversed until A.D. 280, it seems to me probable that
Nuits and Beaune were planted to vines after A.D. 280.
Could the vineyards have got into the state described after
only 32 years? Yes.

Indeed, to carry the argument a stage further, the very
condition of the vineyards was evidence, but nobody seems
to have realized it (significant, for it shows their want of
experience), that the vineyards were not much older, at the
outside, than the more elderly among the crowd of *vignerons*
who listened to their spokesman wheedling tax concessions
out of the emperor. Note that the only remedy the rhetor
can think of is to remove the vineyards elsewhere, and he
says that they cannot do this because there is no room.
But the fact is that had the vineyards been more than a
century old the growers could not have failed to notice that
the platform of roots which was causing all the trouble was
rotting away nicely and forming new, loamy soil for covering the *provins*. For that is what happens. There is a critical
and troublesome period when the vines are less than half
a century old, and then a sort of balance is established between the rate at which the oldest roots decay and the rate
at which new ones are formed, and the vines in such condition start living well off their own decaying substance.
Now had the vine-growers of Autun been practising viticulture as long as they pretended when their rhetor said
that they could no longer recall the age of their vines, they
would have known that this was so, and that once this process is well under way, propagation by *provignage* can go on,
for all anyone knows, indefinitely (in the absence of *Phylloxera* and its corollary, virus disease). The old, pre-
Phylloxera growers hold that a vineyard was immortal, if the
viticulteurs had the trick of rooting *provins* at such a rate as
would balance the dying off of the older stocks.

In short, the famous vineyards between Lyon in the south
and Chablis in the north began their career about 1,700
years ago.

CHABLIS

Chablis is a small, undistinguished, pleasant town which
exists by, for and from its famous white wine. There are no

'sights' to see, the nearest is probably the superb thirteenth-century Gothic cathedral at Auxerre. And this is fitting, for what matters throughout Burgundy is wine. There are, of course, other things to be seen and admired, but even the scenery has, at least through the principal Côtes, been ruined by wine: tree-felling, the excessively symmetrical planting of the vines, and the great main road which goes slap through between the Côtes and the plain, all make for unsightliness. The palate, the imagination and the stomach are what this province caters for, rather than the eye, until we get into the Beaujolais. However, it is a sort of ribbon development, and the hinterland is pleasant enough.

The vineyards of Chablis were formerly much more extensive, but the slopes have serious climatic disadvantages: between about 1870 and 1900 there were eight years of early autumn or late spring frosts, in some years both, with only the months of June, July and August being entirely frost-free. At the same time came the first attacks of the American vine fungus, *Plasmopara viticola*, the friend of the copper magnates, since copper is the effective fungicide. This was not realized at once, and the growers were helpless. The fungus will run through a whole vineyard in a few days of suitably damp, fairly warm weather, leaving the vines defoliated and apt to die in the coming winter. Finally, as if frost and fungus were not enough, came *Phylloxera*, aptly called *vastatrix*, the devastator. The Chablis vineyard was wiped out. And when, by the invention of bordeaux-mixture fungicide, an improvement in the weather, and the trick of grafting French vines on to American roots, replanting became possible, it was too expensive for many former growers. Hence the shrunken vineyards of today.

If I explain the grading of Chablis wines, I shall have explained that of all the Burgundies, for the rules are identical throughout the region of the *Appellation*.

BURGUNDY
'*Village' Wines*

The good, but not outstanding, wines grown in the vineyards round a small town or village according to the

Appellation d'Origine rules governing varieties, density of planting, pruning and vinification, are called by the village name: thus *Chablis Village*. A village name on a Burgundy therefore means that the wine in the bottle is one step up from the ordinary 'Burgundy'.

First-growth Village Wines

The best sites in each village group are selected to yield a wine of the same character as the village wine, but of superior quality. Since the sites in question are chosen for their superior exposure to the sun, they are called *climats*. The *climats* names are local parochial ones. To designate a wine of this *premier crus* class, the name of its climat is tacked on to the village name: thus e.g. Chablis Caucoupin, Chablis Les Lys, etc.

Grand crus *Wines*

The *grands crus* are not village wines at all. All of them come from a vineyard on one of the famous *Côtes*, the site being chosen for superlative exposure, soil and, empirically, by the quality of the wine it produces. The *grands crus* of Burgundy are entitled to call themselves by the name of the vineyard, and no other wine may in any circumstances use that name.

All the wines of Chablis have the same basic character because they are all made from the same grape, whether they be *village, climat* or *grands crus*. This grape is the Chardonnay, often and incorrectly called Pinot blanc. The Chablis are extremely dry, delicate, flinty . . . the taste referred to by this word is as unmistakable as it is indescribable without giving the wrong impression. Dr. Jules Guyot thought them remarkable for, among other things, their whiteness. This has always puzzled me, for to me they seem to be yellow with greenish lights in their limpidity. These Chablis qualities are more or less developed according to the grading of the wine, for in no wine is the scale of improvement from bottom to top more remarkable. For this reason, if for no other, Chablis is an admirable tutor in the judgement of white wines.

The *grands crus* of Chablis come exclusively from the following six vineyards:

Vaudesir, yielding Vaudesir and also Moutonne
Preuses
Grenouilles
Bougros
Valmur
Blanchots

The first-growth vineyards are all on the slopes down to one or other bank of the river Serein. They are, Beaurroy, Troène, Côte-de-Lechet, Les Lys, Sèche, Châtain, Vaillon Beugnon, Melinots, Butteaux, Les Forêts, Montmain, Vosgros, Vaugirard and Roncières, all on the left bank; and on the right, Montée de Tonnerre, Chapelot, Pied d'Aloup, Mont de Milieu, Vaucoupin, Vaulorent, Fourchanne, Côte-de-Fontenay and Vaupulant.

Chablis is a good centre from which to visit the region, much pleasanter here and as far as Dijon, than it is farther south. The food is very good indeed without being wildly extravagant, as it tends to become on the Côte d'Or. On the whole, avoid *les routiers,* the famous pull-ups for car-men, as they were originally, on the great main roads. They were very good and cheap when the black market was still the best source of foodstuffs, for lorry drivers have advantages denied to other men in the matter of transporting black-market produce; and until fashion and the *Guide Michelin* discovered them. But notoriety, or fame if you like, has gone to their heads, and too many are now pretentious and dear: naturally there are exceptions, and if you know or hear of one, then by all means go to it. There is an older and safer rule for finding good restaurants and comfortable, unpretentious hotels in France: find out where the majority of commercial travellers go and go there yourself. The heirs of *l'Illustre Gaudissart* know how to take care of themselves.

While on the subject of food, not very far south of Chablis by motoring standards, is the pleasant small town of Avallon, and there, at the Hotel de la Poste, is one of the half-dozen finest restaurants in Europe, and therefore in the world, for Europeans are the only people who know how to eat, unless the art still survives in China. In making this claim for the Hotel de la Poste I am clearly sticking my neck out: in the first place I shall be accused of being in the management's pay. I am not, actually, but there is always hope. In the second place, nothing changes quicker than the standard of cooking in restaurants, excepting the weather in England; a place which was superb one week is apt to be very bad the next, if the two weeks in question are about the time when the restaurateur discovers that his reputation having been made by the quality of his meals, he can go on living on it while abandoning that quality. It depends on whether the man is a get-rich-quick tradesman or a crafts-man interested in his work. However, I hope that the Hotel de la Poste is still as good as when I visited it. If you go there, do not look at the prices on the menu; they will spoil your appetite and you may not realize, until after your meal, that there is some cooking, just as there is some painting and writing and music, which cannot be valued for money. Just take a great deal of cash with you and pay cheerfully, for you will have had a gastronomic experience of the highest order, and this can happen only two or three times in the lifetime of ordinary men, so that it is worth what it costs. It may seem to you absurd to pay a couple of pounds for a single course of a four- or five-course meal. But you are not paying simply for the raw materials; and you have no way of estimating the value of what you *are* paying for —skilled labour. You would not, presumably, consider the value of a painting to be that of its canvas and paint. The Avallon place is also a good one in which to sample one or two of the really great Burgundies, for they have, as I recall it, an admirable wine-list.

If you are one of those puritans who needs a spiritual or educational excuse for self-indulgence, you can make not Avallon, but Vezelay, the object of your excursion from Chablis, and tell yourself that you have to eat somewhere en route and might just as well do so at the de la Poste. Vezelay is certainly not to be missed; the great, echoing monastery basilica, growing, as it seems to do, out of the quaint, steep village on its hill, is one of the most strikingly sited, beautiful buildings in France, dominating a panorama so enormous and so full of fascinating detail, that I could hardly turn from it to the archeological and architectural interest of the church itself.

Apart from Chablis, the other wines of the Yonne entitled to call themselves Burgundy are made, as to whites, from Chardonnay or Sacy grapes; as to red, from three strains of Pinot locally known as Noirien, Liebault and Beurot, and from two entirely local and rapidly vanishing *cépages*, César (*syn*. Romain) which produces a late, black grape yielding a full-bodied, subtle wine, hardish when young but softening with age, and Tressot (*syn*. Tresseau, Verot, Verreau, *et alia*), yielding a wine of which I can say nothing excepting that it has the same virtue as an Irish pot of tea, it is so strong a mouse could trot on it. Susceptibility to the fungus disease *oidium* is putting this vine out of cultivation. All these wines can be had quite cheaply in the villages and all make good luncheon picnic drinks excepting Tressot, if you can identify it, which is apt to put you to sleep at the wheel.

From Chablis you drive to Dijon. It is a city I should not want to live in, for it is curiously noisy. It is, however, one of those towns which are beautiful to look down upon. The part of it I know best is the railway station in the small hours, for when at school in Switzerland I used to return after holidays in England on the Simplon-Orient Express, and, without fail, be woken up at some horrible hour by the train stopping at Dijon. There, peering out of my carriage window, resentful at being roused to all the discomfort and gritty nastiness of a second-class carriage after hours and hours of travelling, I would see Dijon—a long, an interminably long, platform looking cold and dismal under yellow lights; piles of luggage which looked as if it had been there since the dawn of time and would remain there until time ran out; a dozen or so conscript soldiers, sleeping propped on their kitbags and looking like 'huddled shapes'. Poor Dijon, it is hardly fair to judge it with that for an introduction! And it must be admitted that it probably has the best ordinary restaurants in France. I do not, this time, mean restaurants for *haute cuisine,* but the ordinary place you drop into because it is nearest and the menu in the window is 850 frs., or even 500 frs. I never found a bad one, and it is possible to eat well for twelve shillings. Do I hear someone say that by English standards that is too much? Make no such comparison. Certainly it is possible to eat cheaper in England than anywhere else without being actually poisoned, and in fact being quite adequately nourished. But quality for quality, penny for penny, food in England is much dearer than it is in France. Your twelve shillings Dijon meal would cost you 30s. in England and be not quite so good. As for your 4s. 6d. London luncheon, you simply could not get it in France, it would not be thought adequate as human food. You can, of course, eat as badly in France as anywhere; the old days when any small restaurant was reliable are gone. But as a rule, this badness is high-class expensive badness, and you will be surrounded by English and Americans and Germans praising the shocking and pretentious food for which they will cheerfully pay more than they would pay for half a week's meals at home.

The Burgundian wine-route is N6, about as peaceful as our own A1. Taking it south out of Dijon, you pass through the viticultural *commune* of Fixin; you pass through it, that is the point. Why? I have no idea, and so little originality have I that it never occurred to me to stop. Everyone passes through Fixin, and I cannot recall ever knowingly drinking any of its wine, so for all I know it is the best in Burgundy. It has not that reputation, however. The first *great* vineyard you come to is Gevrey-Chambertin, the northernmost, and as some think the most distinguished, of the Côte d'Or.

* * * * * *

The whole Côte d'Or is comprised in about 20,000 acres of vineyard, but only half of this area produces wine of *Appellation Controllée* rank, while the *grand crus* vineyards are only a fraction of this half, none of them producing as much wine as they could sell, by a long chalk. The difference between one great wine and another from this series of slopes is that the soil of the whole Côte is very diverse, although, as in Chablis, a lot of the subsoil is chalk. Density of plantation is about 4,000 plants to the acre, and stakes and wires are provided for tying in the fruit-bearing shoots.

We are at Gevrey-Chambertin: from north to south the *côtes* into which the whole Côte d'Or is divided are three:

1. *The Côte de Nuits*

Its 'villages' are Gevrey-Chambertin, Morey St. Denis, Chambolle-Musigny, Vougeot, Vosne-Romanée, Nuits St. Georges, all on the right-hand side of the road as you drive south, and all with both 'village' and 'climate' wines. Its *grands crus* are, e.g. of Gevrey-Chambertin, *Clos de Bèze, Chambertin*; of Morey, *Clos de Tart*, a superb wine; of Vougeot, *Clos Vougeot*, its 120 acres of vineyards still within the wall built by the Cistercian monks, but now owned by scores of smallholders.

There is, in the château at Clos Vougeot, a museum of Burgundy wine. And the château is the headquarters of a bibulous Order, the *Confrérie des Chevaliers du Tastevin*, whose motto is *Jamais en vain. Toujours en vin*, a horrible pun. By name, *taste-vin*, this is a wine-tasting fraternity, for *taster* is the old form of the modern *tâter*, which, in one of its meanings, has the same sense as our own word to taste—it is, of course, the same word. The brotherhood put on some very spectacular shows, and although perhaps priggishly I think a parade and fuss about wine rather a pity—for it should be the daily and commonplace drink of all civilized men who have access to it—the fun is as harmless as any publicity stunt of the kind can be. And if it is *not* a publicity stunt, then I apologize . . . but all that dressing-up! *Voyons, messieurs!*

For many English wine-lovers, Clos Vougeot is the 'greatest' red wine in the world. In point of fact there is no such thing, and in any case other Burgundies are often quite obviously better wines, the *grands crus* of Morey St. Denis being outstanding. Vosne-Romanée has another of these 'greatest' Burgundies—Romanée Conti, which comes from fewer than 20,000 vines in all, for the vineyard is about 4½ acres. So true is it that the quality of a wine is closely associated with the soil of the vineyard, that attempts to increase the annual output of Romanée Conti by planting

land on the periphery of this tiny vineyard failed. Or so I
have been told.

Last village of the Côte de Nuits is Nuits St. Georges,
where the vineyard is more extensive, something like a
thousand acres.

All the important Côte de Nuits wines are red, and all
long-lived as Burgundies go. But even a *grand cru* of
Gevrey-Chambertin, which matures more slowly than the
wines to the south of it, will not go on improving in bottle
for anything like as long as a great claret. This does not,
repeat not, mean that Burgundies are not 'as good as' red
Bordeaux. No such comparison is viable; it simply does not
mean anything.

Aloxe-Corton, the first vineyard of the Côte de Beaune, is
north of Beaune itself, but the rest of the vineyards lie
south of the town, a prosperous, bustling place, very agreeable to poke about in, with rewarding back streets and a
score of nicely composed townscapes. It was formerly the
ducal capital. It is now one vast wine cellar; too vast by
some accounts, which declare that more wine goes out of
them, in bottles nobly labelled, than ever grew on the
Côte d'Or. A good deal of 'Burgundy' is said, in short, to
come from Languedoc or Algeria. The implication is that
the excess of demand for the great Burgundies over supply,
the certainty that most buyers of such wines go by the label,
not the taste, and the immense success of the Burgundy
mystique which keeps the price high even if the quantity of wine
is stretched, have all been too much for the wine-merchants
of Beaune. The undeniable fact that a great deal of wine
comes into the region, especially in lean years, is explained
thus: 'We poor Burgundians make great wine for other
people and are so ill-paid for it that we cannot afford to
drink it ourselves, and have to import *vin ordinaire* from the
places where it is produced in bulk. Do not brutally accuse
us of fraud, but pity us.' Echoes of the rhetor's speech to
Constantine!

What is there to be said about all this? That we get the
tradesmen we deserve, and that I have a great respect for
Burgundian business acumen. After all, those who know
can always get the real thing, using the palate to judge by.

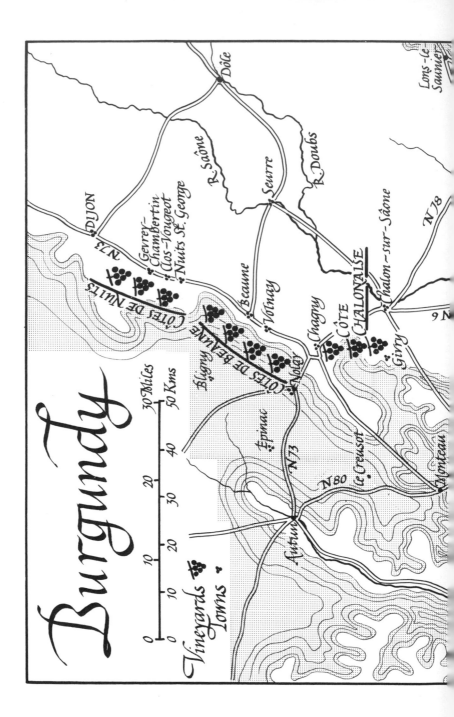

Burgundy

Vineyards 🍇
Towns •

Miles: 0 10 20 30
Kms: 0 10 20 30 40 50

DIJON
N.73
Gevrey–Chambertin
Clos–Vougeot
Nuits St. George
CÔTES DE NUITS
R. Saône
Dôle
Seurre
R. Doubs
Beaune
Volnay
CÔTES DE BEAUNE
Pommard
Bligny
Épinac
N.73
N 80
Autun
Le Creusot
Chagny
Givry
CÔTE CHALONAISE
Chalon–sur–Saône
N.78
N 6
Montceau
Lons–le–Saunier

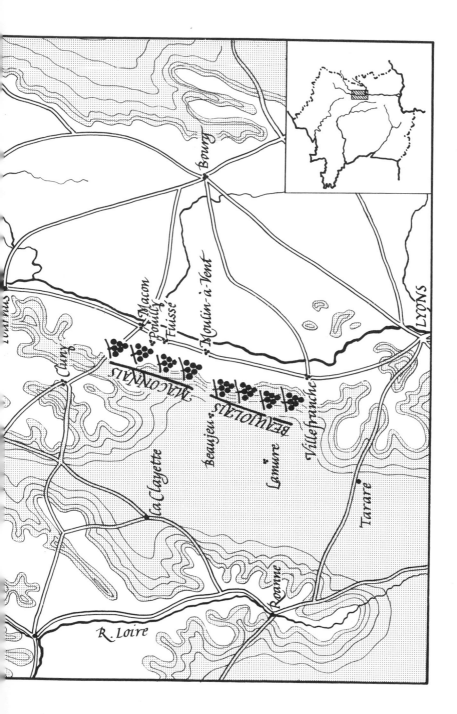

Not Chambertin, always; nor, always, Romanée Conti, for there is so little of both, and of that so much goes to favoured friends of the growers. But usually Vougeot or Nuits. And as for those who do not know, and who are paying Burgundy prices for a good, wholesome blend of Burgundy and Algerian, they are quite happy. True, they will not develop a wine-palate, but for the most part they could not do that in any case, for they drink hard liquor, and they smoke like factory chimneys. Besides, we have been conditioned every day since the invention of advertising to ignore the evidence of our mere senses, the palate or the nose or the eyes, and go by the slogan. So that most drinkers of Burgundy on occasion are perfectly happy if the label is right and the price reassuringly high, and if the wine has a reasonably good bouquet and tastes nice. The 'stretchers' of wine in the cellars of Beaune are honest after their fashion; what they put into the bottle is not, it is true, what the label will imply or even state downright. But it is good, carefully blended wine, incomparably better and more wholesome to drink than the billions of gallons of sugared rubbish, considered by some people to be more or less poisonous, annually consumed all over the world as soft drinks, and scandalously free from taxation. The eating and drinking of half the world's population has become 'Platonic'; we consume what we are told (at enormous expense of spirit and cash in a vast waste of shame and paper) as wholesome. And, because we have faith, we are nourished. At least the stuff we buy from the fraudulent wine-blender as a *grand cru* Burgundy is wine. What is the stuff we buy as lemonade?

Moreover, flying in the face of the whole spirit of modern food and drink commerce, the French authorities wage constant war on the fraudulent blenders, and these sharp operators themselves are in a small minority. For, in more senses than one, there is truth in wine and the amount of such fraud practised is in nothing like proportion to the temptation.

As for your own behaviour: if, upon tasting a wine bought as a Chablis, a Mâcon or a Beaujolais[1] of a specific

---

[1] Denis Morris, in the book already quoted, says that these are the three most commonly stretched.

Appellation and paid for accordingly, you know enough to tell that the wine has been stretched, then make a hell of a fuss. If you do not know enough to judge, then you will drink up happily and be none the wiser and will have enriched a lot of deserving people in the wine trade, helping to support them in the affluence their vocation deserves.

Beaune: its greatness, of course, is its great *Hospice*. This was built by Nicholas Rollin, Chancellor to Phillipe le Bon, duke of Burgundy, in the middle of the fifteenth century, as an asylum for the aged and infirm poor of the town and countryside whom, as that shrewd politician Louis XI of France pointed out, were numerous and in need of such help owing to the extortions of their 'benefactor'. The spectacle of a very successful self-made man giving back with his right hand what his left has been busy stealing for a lifetime is one with which we are perfectly familiar; and in any case Louis, a sanctimonious rogue if ever one sat on a throne, was in no position to sneer. Rollin might perfectly well have kept his money in his pocket, or squandered it on girls, or, much worse, on the fifteenth-century equivalent of H-bombs. As it is we have the Hospice, an imposing building of great beauty, great architectural interest, dominating the town of Beaune in every quarter. As a building, as a museum of oenological objects of art and vertu, and as a centre of commerce, the Hospice de Beaune is well worth a visit.

2. The Côte de Beaune

The Côte de Beaune is known for both its red and its white wines. The great names in reds are Beaune, Pommard, Volnay, Aloxe-Corton, Savigny and Santenay. And in whites, Mersault, Corton-Charlemagne and Montrachet.

From south of Beaune, where most of these vineyards are to be found, the country begins to become more agreeable to look at for, from the high places of the Côte, one catches glimpses of wooded hills to the south, a foretaste of the Mâconnais and the Beaujolais.

Aloxe-Corton is comprised in numerous small vineyards carefully sited so as to be fully exposed all day long, producing a full-bodied wine which acquires a superb bouquet with age. Wines of the same kind are produced by Volnay and by Pommard, both so well known to the English toper who annually consumes a fair proportion of their output, that little need be said about them. Savigny wines are a little lighter and more delicate than these three; one could express it by saying that Savigny is a Burgundy to drink in summer, Pommard and Volnay in winter. Or Savigny at lunch, Pommard at dinner. At the risk of treating the reds of Beaune with too little respect, I prefer to give my attention, in this mid-section of the Burgundy vineyard, to the tremendous whites.

The most northerly of these come from Aloxe-Corton; they are Corton-Charlemagne and Charlemagne. Corton-Charlemagne is an excellent example of the limited quantities of these great wines available to the ordinary drinker, who will be lucky to get so much as a bottle: its annual output averages about 40,000 bottles more or less. It is a golden wine, substantial, 12° alcohol, rich in subtle flavours often too fancifully described. It should be not less than two years old before you drink it; not more than six; for outside those limits it is not itself.

Next of the whites as you go south along N6, are those of Mersault—all the places I have named or shall name in this chapter have, as explained, *village, climat* and *grands crus* wines. For my taste the *grands crus* of Mersault are the finest substantial white wines in the world, wines which are white but have something of the weight of reds. Happily, they are numerous:

Two Genevrières, Les Genevrières-Dessus
Les Genevrières-Dessous,

or, as we should say in England, Upper Genevrières and Nether Genevrières.

Three Perrières,	Les Perrières-Dessus
	Les Perrières-Dessous
	Aux Perrières
Two Poruzots,	Le Poruzot
	Le Poruzot-Dessus

and then, the names full of local, bucolic charm, La Pièce-sous-le-Bois, Sous-le-dos-d'ane, Les Caillerets, Les Petures,

La Jeannelotte, La Goutte d'Or, Les Cras, Les Santenots-du-Milieu, and Les Santenots-Blancs. The wines of all these *pièces* are dry but substantial, alcoholic, fruity, golden-yellow shot with greenish lights.

South of the Mersaults are the wines of Puligny-Montrachet. Both Montrachet and Montrachet-Chevalier are among the greatest of wines, but as the vineyard is only about twenty acres in extent, and the entire annual output about 4,000 bottles, most of which are kept by the growers or sold to their pals, and as far more wine labelled Montrachet seems to be sold every year than could be produced if the vineyard were ten times the size, it is difficult for the ordinary drinker, even with a pocket full of money, to get any. However, in case you do get the chance, there are five *grands crus,* all of more or less equal merit, although Montrachet itself is the *tete de cuvée,* the *primus inter pares* . . . in short, the reputed best.

> Montrachet
> Montrachet-Chevalier
> Bâtard Montrachet
> Bienvenues-Montrachet
> Criots-Bâtard-Montrachet

The Chassagne-Montrachet vineyard, next in geographical order, includes parts of the last three in the above list, some other and lesser known whites, and some *grands crus* red wines which are equal, in my personal opinion, to all but Chambertin of the Nuits reds. One, La Romanée, is not to be confused with the Nuits Romanée, which is very much dearer and not all that better, if it *is* better.

3. *The Côte-Chalonnaise*

The 'red' *communes* of the Côte Chalonnaise are Mercurey, Rully and Givry, more scattered than those of the Côte de Beaune. The 'white' *commune* par excellence is Montagny. Mercurey lies off N6 to the west, the road to it being from Chagny. Givry is almost due south of it, and Montagny south-east of Givry, all on the same road which rejoins N6 at Tournus.

The Chalonnaise is an agreeable, rustic piece of country, the farmers and wine-growers being small, in fact very small, holders. The villages are pretty, sometimes distinguished, and the food at the inns consistently good. The smallholders are independent as growers, but for the making and sale of their wine they are grouped in co-operatives. Their *Saône-et-Loire* wines might, I believe, have made a much greater name for themselves than they have done were it not for the fact that they are sold, notably Givry, for the stretching of Beaune wines. There can be no objection to this: for they come from the same grape, climate, and often soil, and are often quite as good. It is simply a question of exploiting the great names of the Côte de Beaune in order to get a better price—'*pas très catholique*', perhaps, as they say in Beaujolais, 'not quite cosher' if you prefer it in New Yorkese; but not very wicked either.

The *premiers crus* of Mercurey, the ones best known by their own name, are Clos-du-Roy, Clos-Voyen, Clos-Marcilly, Clos-des-Fourneaux, Clos-des-Montaigus.

Givry is such an agreeable town in such pleasant, quiet country, that this detour through the *Saône-et-Loire département* makes up for having to by-pass Chalon-sur-Saône, and at Tournus, where you rejoin the main road, you are not far from the ruins of the mother-house of Cluny, whose spiritual, moral and political influence under St. Bernard was so colossal during the Middle Ages. The ruins stand among vineyard country, yet the whole district is so bustling and the traffic of N6 so near that like all ruins, temples and beauty spots outside of great cities, much visited and trodden over, all virtue has gone out of them, and nothing of the pride and glory, and only a trace of the humility which was their basis, remains. It is sad but true that the quality of the past never survives the curiosity of the present. Intelligent interest, or mere gawping sight-seeing, it is all the same: we destroy the delicate quality of the very sights we flock to see by the act of looking at them; and all that is left to us is masonry.

At Tournus the river and the road come together, and there are, a little off the road, good riverside picnic spots before you come to Mâcon. This is another pleasant town, and the still considerable traffic of boats and lighters on the tranquil and embanked Saône recalls a point made earlier—

that commercial vineyards are all on rivers not because of
the suitable slopes only, but because, in the centuries when
the vineyards of France were being planted, rivers, not
roads, provided the cheapest and best means of freight
transport. The Saône still carries a certain amount of wine
from the vineyards which slope down to Mâcon. And, like
the river, many of the town's oldest buildings still serve the
people, while others have been added in every century including our own, making the town one of those places
which are social history in brick and mortar, stone and
timber.

The great tourist 'sight' of the Mâconnais is the Château
Monceau, where Lamartine lived during the second and less
busy part of his life when politics gave way to less mis-
chievous, indeed positively beneficial, activities, such as
writing poetry and prose, contemplating the beautiful surroundings of his house, exercising his taste on that house
and its furniture (still there to be admired), and growing
and making wine. Lamartine should be honoured, if for no
other reason than for having been almost unique among
public men in not merely saying that he preferred a quiet
life in the country but actually going to live such a life.
Visit his house and drink Mâcon to his memory. May all
politicians retire and write poetry and cultivate a vineyard
before the mischief they do becomes intolerable.

The red wines of Mâcon are made in vast quantity and are
not very distinguished. They are, however, perfectly sound,
wholesome, reliable wines, and reasonably cheap. The name
Mâcon on a label, plus a village name, means, as elsewhere in
Burgundy, a superior wine. As for the whites of Mâcon,
they, on the other hand, are very distinguished indeed, and
they include the one I would rather drink with a huge,
grilled Dover sole than any other, that is, Pouilly-Fuissé.
Lugny is another admirable white of the region, the town
being north-west of Mâcon, while Pouilly-Fuissé is south-
west. South of Pouilly-Fuissé, the Mâconnais gets mixed up
with the Beaujolais, since its vineyards almost march with
Juliènas and St. Amour, both Beaujolais *grands crus*. The
premiers crus of Pouilly are Fuissé, Solutré, Pouilly, Vergison
and Chaintre.

Before leaving the Mâconnais, make a point of trying to taste some of the 'hybrid' vine wines which are grown there in a few places, not of course on classified slopes, mostly in *Saône-et-Loire* and in *Ain*, in the valley of the Saône. They are grown to provide the owners with wine for their own drinking, come frost or rain. There is said to be still a certain amount of the vine called *Noah* growing in these parts. If you get a chance to taste the wine of this early *V. labrusca* hybrid, do so, and you will know what the bad name of the P.D. vines was founded on. On the other hand, as well as such moderately good varieties as Seibel 7053, some of the more enterprising peasants have planted such relative novelties as Ravat 6; if you can taste carefully vinted wine from this hybrid, you will understand why the supporters of the P.D. vines protest that P.D. wines should not be judged by the products of Noah and the like. I have had, in the charming house of that great advocate of the *nouvelle viticulture*, M. Gerard Marot, in Poitiers, wine of Ravat 6 which towers above a great deal of the sound, ordinary wine made from vinifera grapes; and the hybrid vine men claim no more than that their vines should do the donkey work of providing *vin courant*.

4. *The Beaujolais*

Is Beaujolais, like Nuits, Beaune and Mâcon, 'Burgundy'? The books say yes and the people loudly deny it. I think they are right. Beaujolais is a different kind of wine. For one thing it does not improve after three years; it is lighter, less 'serious'. And it does not *need* to improve. It is perfect as it is at three years of age. And thus whoever insists on vintage Beaujolais is an ass and deserves to be defrauded, as he certainly will be, by an enterprising merchant perfectly willing to provide what he is asked for and to get well paid for it.

The Beaujolais consists of a lot of rather confusing granitic hills in the extreme south of the Saône-et-Loire *département*, about Villefranche-sur-Saône. Its villages and small towns, perched on top of the hills, have a quality of remoteness and concentration on their own business which is very soothing. I forget which one of them is supposed to be Clochemerle, but it is a tribute to the power of good writing that probably more English people know something about the life of a Beaujolais wine village than about any other wine community in the world, because of the enormous success enjoyed by Chevalier's books. However, the visitor to these granitic hills and their hilltop towns should remember that good comedy creates its own ideal world out of a reality less striking. Do not look too hard for Clochemerle, for you will not find it. Do not, in fact, go to Beaujolais with Clochemerle in mind, for unless the magnification power and colour of your spectacles are the same as Chevalier's own, you will be disappointed. But I am far from saying that *Clochemerle* is no more than good entertainment; it is pointed, it reveals a great deal about French small-town politics, love and commerce. But the trick is not worked by copying from life.

Beaujolais has its *grands crus* and its village wines. There is also just Beaujolais or *Beaujolais Supérieur* for drinking from the wood—your picnic wine, or for that matter your restaurant wine served *en carafe*.

The authorities of the *Appellation d'Origine* offices list as *grands crus* the following wines which may improve in bottles up to five years, but certainly no longer: Moulin-à-Vent; Juliènas; Fleurie; Chiroubles; Chenas; Morgan; and Brouilly. For my taste, Juliènas is the best of these wines; they differ from each other a good deal, but not very much from year to year. The general expert opinion seems to be that Moulin-à-Vent is the *tête de cuvée*.

*   *   *   *   *   *

As to the *cépages* of Burgundy. The most important is the almost ubiquitous Pinot noir, and after that several of the other Pinots. Locally, it is called *Noirien*. We have already noted Chardonnay, Sacy, Tressot and César, in Chablis, where there is also a good deal of Gamay, there yielding a wine of no distinction. This same Gamay, however, despite all the abuse poured on it by the great Guyot, is a very good vine if planted in austere soils. It is so planted in the Beaujolais, where it gives of its best. A very interesting light is thrown on the adaptability of this variety by the splendid late-nineteenth-century experiment in Welsh viticulture carried out with one of the Gamays in Glamorganshire by the Marquis of Bute. In 1875 he planted fourteen acres below castle Coch with this vine; and a few years later a further nine acres elsewhere. Mr. Pettigrew, in charge of the experiment and writing seventeen years later, said that more or less wine had been made almost every year between 1877 and 1904, with a couple of failures only. Note that these included eight very bad years in France. 'The vintage of 1881 was particularly fine, fetching 60s. a dozen from a Cardiff wine-merchant, some of it being bought by Dr. Lawson Tait, a famous connoisseur and some resold at auction for 115s. a dozen.' The later extension of the vineyard by the nine acres planted at Swanbridge was soon yielding 12,000 bottles of wine a year. Unhappily, the first German war put an end to an experiment which might have had some interesting economic consequences for that part of Wales.

So much for Gamay: it is down in the ampelographies as being *maturité de première époque hâtive*, an early and quick-ripening variety, which should therefore be suitable for Kent; but it is not one of the varieties we have tried yet.

For white Burgundies, as well as Chardonnay, two other *cépages* are grown. Chardonnay is variously known as Pinot blanc, Noirien blanc, Beaunois, Auxerrois blanc, Plant doré blanc; and it is not, in fact, a Pinot. There *is* a true white Pinot, which originated as a mutant on Pinot noir; but it is inferior to Chardonnay. The next white *cépage* is Aligoté whose grapes, when quite ripe, are grizzled grey and pink, for which reason one of its synonyms is Plant gris. As a rule its wine is not up to much, but where the vine is grown on a classified site and its output limited to 450 gallons an acre in order to raise the quality of the fruit, it has the right to an *Appellation*, to wit, *Bourgogne-Aligoté*.

The Melon vine is an interesting variety already met with in Anjou. In Burgundy it is never planted on classified slopes, nor, nowadays, in the real wine *communes* at all, but only by farmers in other parts of Burgundy for their own domestic wine-making. Its name derives from the melon-leaf shape of the foliage. In Burgundy its wine is thought poor. But since this is the Muscadet of the Loire valley, it

clearly behaves differently farther west, a striking example
of the need to suit *cépage* to soil.

Reaching the south of Beaujolais and finally Lyon, we are
at the end of Burgundy. At Lyon the Saône is joined by the
Rhône. Before going south of Lyon to the Côtes de Rhône
wines, however, we will make a detour into a much less
famous wine-province . . . Franche-Comté.

CHAPTER EIGHT

THE WINES OF THE JURA

THE Franche-Comte is that part of France which marches with Switzerland. It is a long, narrow *massif* of mountains, the Jura, some of whose beautiful high passes are like back doors into Switzerland, whose lonely frontier guards, with two or three Customs men living in a small cottage, have a pleasantly liberal attitude to the few motorists who go through their hands. They are more interested in a chat about where you have come from and are going to, the scandalous cost of living, the harsh weather of the past winter and, surprisingly, the glorious spring flowers of their mountains. Surprisingly because to most French people wild flowers are just wild flowers. It was a Customs man at one of these passes who directed us to the best banks of wild daffodils and narcissi, and told us what orchids were to be found in the pass. For the holidaymaker who is more interested in magnificent mountain scenery, in quiet and lovely places beside a stream, in flowers and mountain meadows and the reserved but friendly shepherds of such country, than in towns and beaches, the Jura has a great deal to recommend it. France, with two and a half times the surface area of Britain and ten million fewer people, with a diversity of mountain ranges and a wealth of rivers great and small, is unquestionably the most perfect country in Europe for the nature-lover. And as its small towns and great cities provide, incomparably, for the creature comforts, one can have it both ways.

The principal vineyards of the Jura are among the foothills of those mountains, beginning at about Arbois in the north and extending southwards to join the Beaujolais vineyards at St. Amour. So that the visitor who is already at

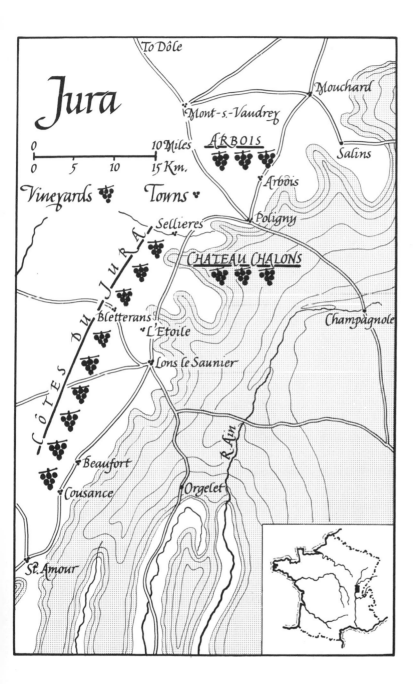

St. Amour for the Beaujolais wines is on the threshold of the Jura wines, the 'frontier' being, roughly, the main road between Besançon and Lyon.

As if to offset its many charms, the Jura is distinguished for what I think must be the most singular gastronomic atrocity known to *cuisine*, although I had better add that many people admire it, eat it with relish, thereafter sleep without suffering nightmare; and that it is supposed to have nourished the men of the mountain Resistance who, hunted by the German uniformed thugs, had often to do their eating in a hurry and vanish. This dish is *fondu*, an infamous comestible of cooked cheese. If the English were half as good as the French at promoting the fame of their national and regional dishes, then Welsh rarebit, a cheese dish beyond comparison superior to either *fondu* or that other nastiness, Neapolitan *pizza*, would be bringing thousands of gourmets to Britain every year.

Fondu, if you must try it, is eaten standing. The victims gather about a table on which is placed a chafing-dish heater with a large bowl on it. Into this bowl is melted a large quantity of Gruyère cheese, mixed with condiments and a dash of kirsch, with or without egg stirred into it. Each of the prospective candidates for indigestion is provided with a long fork and a plateful of small bits of bread. A bit of bread is impaled on the fork, dipped into and twisted in the *fondu*, and the resultant glutinous lump is then eaten dangerously hot. As the consistency is that of semi-molten rubber, chewing is impossible and bolting inevitable. *Hinc illae lacrimae!* Whoever drops his bread into the bowl instead of getting it out smothered with *fondu* has to stand another bottle of the light, fragrant Jura wine drunk with this dish, and which is the only agreeable part of the operation.

While on the subject, the Swiss, across the passes, also have a dish they call *fondu*, which is a really wicked tourist-bait racket. It is a means of getting the customers to do their own cooking while charging them more than if it had been done for them. It, too, is a gastronomic abomination and much less forgivable because instead of being a dirt-cheap way of ridding oneself of an expensive appetite for a couple of days, it is hideously expensive. Again there is the bowl on the heater, but this time it is full of boiling fat. And what the customers are supplied with is not a plate of bread cubes, but a plate of raw beef-steak cubes. Also on the table are about a score of small dishes containing a diversity of incompatible sauces. The diners impale a cube of meat on the fork, hold it in the fat until it is fried, dip it into several conflicting sauces and eat it. In Zurich the privilege of doing this costs about thirty bob a head. Of course, it is a lot of fun, everyone is very merry and facetious. But as food . . . it really will not do.

The small, quiet towns of the Jura, like Salins, are some of the pleasantest, though undistinguished, in France, very unpretentious, with nothing to show, but also nothing to offend. Altogether a part of France well worthy of being much better known than it is.

There is, of course, nothing so grand as a *route du vin*, but the convenient road to follow from Arbois is N83 to Poligny, where it crosses the Orain, and then N5, to Lons-le-Saunier and St. Amour and, finally, to Lyon. The vine-yards occur at irregular intervals along this line, in small fields on very steep slopes well protected from the cold quarters, and their vines are crowded close. Thus, although their altitude is between 750 and 1,000 feet above sea-level, with high mountains rising behind them, the grapes are well placed to ripen, and the wines produced admirable of their mountain kind, a kind for which I, personally, have a special liking.

The *cépages* principally planted in the Jura are Traminer, which we have already met with but which is here called either Savagnin, Nature blanc or Fromenté—depending on the parish—and whose grapes are rarely harvested until late October; Chardonnay, here confusingly called Melon d'Arbois, although it is not the Melon of Burgundy nor the Muscadet of the Loire, nor even the Pinot blanc. These two *cépages* are for white wines, or rather, as we shall see, yellow wines. For the reds they plant Poulsard or Plant d'Arbois, the latter so poor in colour that it yields not a true red wine but a *peau d'oignon*, a reddish brown. And, finally, an old, rapidly dying *cépage*, Trousseau, which does not ripen well and has its grapes too tightly packed in the bunch, thus giving rise to fungus troubles.

About Arbois, the wine to drink is the *rosé d'Arbois*, a fresh, lively, quite strong wine which should be drunk cooled as if it were a white, and which is one of the finest *rosé* wines in France, better, in my opinion, than *rosé* d'Anjou which has a sort of metallic sweetness, and much better than that wicked wine, Tavel. White wines of pleasant quality are also made locally, and likewise both yellow and 'straw' wines. But both of these oenological novelties are better drunk farther south.

For the remarkable yellow wine go and stay a night or two in Château Chalon, farther up the mountains on the river Seille. The vine grown here, and the only grape which yields this *vin jaune* as it should be, is Savagnin, i.e. Traminer. The grapes are often left on the vine until after the first touch of autumn frost has removed the leaves, for frost sweetens grapes by reducing their water-content relative to their sugar. The wine having been made is run into large casks and there, covered with a sort of yeast or mould film, analogous to the *flor* of sherry, it remains for at least six years—a most unusual practice. It may even be left rather longer, in rare cases for ten years. After that it is bottled, and its colour is bright yellow. The object of the exercise is, however, the very peculiar taste, so indescribable that the people of Château Chalon simply say that it has a *gout de jaune,* that is, that 'it tastes yellow'. If you think that whimsical, it's not my fault.

To get to the next wine *commune* from Château Chalon you have to return to N83, or else find a side-road, which I never did. And then to make a small detour off the main-road to Lons-le-Saunier, to l'Etoile. Here there are two distinct wines to be tried: the white called Etoile, a fine, clean mountain wine vaguely reminiscent of Frascati, with the same high-spirited quality of being, as it were, about-to-be-sparkling. And, an oenological curiosity, the Etoile *vin de paille*, which is not made *of* straw, but *on* it. It is made from either Traminer or Chardonnay, or both. The grapes are gathered late and laid out on straw-covered racks under a cover and there left slowly to dry and almost to wither, until Christmas. By that time they are *mi-grappe, mi-raisin* quite literally, half grape and half raisin, so that their sugar content reckoned as a percentage may be as high as 35. At Christmas these semi-raisins are pressed and the wine made. Naturally, there is much less of it than there would be if the grapes were pressed when newly harvested. But the alcohol content of the wine is about 17°, instead 11°, and even so the wine, for drinking after meals, not with them, is sweet, *liquoreux* and very fragrant.

Finally, in a curve west of l'Etoile, running from north of St. Amour to south of Poligny, are the Côtes du Jura themselves, where wines of all the kinds made at Arbois, Château Chalon and l'Etoile are made—whites, *rosés*, reds, yellows and straws—but not quite so well as in their places of origin.

East of, and roughly parallel with, the Côtes du Jura and at a distance of seventeen or eighteen miles, flows the river Ain, which gives its name to the *département* between Jura and Haute-Savoie, and where, as already suggested, visitors may get a chance to try 'hybrid' wines for themselves. But this province also produces *Appellation Controllée* wines from small vineyards of Poulsard, Chardonnay, Mondeuse and Roussette vines, in a few of its *communes*—wines totally unknown outside the region but very well worth knowing. They have, of course, much the same qualities and defects as the Jura wines. The least obscure, as to repute, is Seyssel, named after a small town which is actually just over the border into *Ain-et-Haute-Savoie*. Here the white wines, some of them still and some sparkling, are made from Chasselas and Roussette grapes.

The Ain claims these Seyssel wines as its own. But in Haute-Savoie, the next of this group of mountain provinces, they are considered among the wines of Haute-Savoie, and there, since it has become one of the most popular resorts in France, and one of the smartest, visitors are most apt to make their acquaintance.

The scenery of Savoy is some of the most beautiful in France, which is to say, in the world. The principal tourist centre is Annecy, on the lake of that name. South-west of this lake is another, the lac du Bourget, and on its east bank a resort of wealth and fashion with a much longer history than Annecy: Aix-les-Bains, whose medicinal waters are still prescribed for the liverish and rheumatical. The mountain roads of this whole region are good fun to drive on, the landscape is never the same for five minutes at a time, and there are a thousand pleasant places to stop for a picnic, to gather narcissi and a score of other wild flowers in late spring, and to drink interesting 'little' wines. In Aix-les-Bains there is a wide choice of grave and elegant restaurants where the highest of *haute cuisine*, or *cuisine classique*, is practised more or less as a religious rite. The lesser restaurants, contenting themselves with the best of *cuisine bourgeoise*, are likewise dedicated to their vocation. It would seem that the noble cooks of Savoy are all intent upon undoing those livers which their medicinal fellow-countrymen in Aix make a living out of repairing, a happy combination which doubtless explains the continued prosperity of that handsome town. As for Annecy, it offers every kind of water sport, a fine summer climate rarely oppressively hot; in winter, ski slopes are not far away.

In addition to the wines of Seyssel, Savoy produces another which is entitled to an *Appellation d'Origine*—Crépy; and a number of VDQS wines, known either as *Vins de Savoie* or, after the vine, *Roussette de Savoie*. The best among these are entitled to use the *commune* name as well: the best known of these *communes* are Abymes, Montmélian, Chantage, Marignan, Apremen; there are others. As you will rarely, if ever, find these wines, produced in quite small quantities, outside their own country, it is a good idea to insist upon drinking them when you are there, either in bottle or from the wood.

The fact that Savoy is not one of the really important viticultural provinces and has not been subject to the same pressures in favour of standardization, means that its *encépagement* is much more diverse. It is true that the three principal noble varieties are much grown there—Pinot, Gamay and Chardonnay. But there is also a number of interesting old local *cépages*, some of them of great antiquity. Consequently the wine differs in interesting ways from parish to parish; and sometimes it is poor stuff, so that a taste of it is sufficient to indicate why the growers in other wine districts have turned more and more to one or two proved varieties. Where, for example, Savoyanne, also called Mondeuse, is still grown, the wine is harsh and acid when drawn from the wood, although a bottle five or six years old can be surprisingly good. Much the same is true of wines made from Aguzelle grapes. Here and there you may find small vineyards of huge, gnarled old plants clinging to a hillside, the variety being Hibou noir, black owl, also called Hivernais, for the lateness of its harvest. Elsewhere it has other, equally whimsical, names. Heaven knows why it is still cultivated: it matures its fruit far too late for these mountains, and its wine is invariably acid and weak in alcohol simple because the grapes used are never ripe. Durif, or Pinot de Romans, grown in Savoy, in the Isère and in the Drome, is another bad *cépage* for this kind of country, yet the people cling to it, probably because having a plantation of old vines, they simply cannot be bothered to replant. Its wine is hard, acid and without character. The Corbeaune vine is another in the same class, but a plant allowed to grow very large, enormously fruitful. All these produce the red wine drunk by the locals and rarely sold beyond the village *bistros*. I have no hesitation whatever in saying that replanting with the best PD vines of the *premier époque* would yield more and much better wine with less trouble.

This fact has indeed been grasped in the Isère *département* where 20,000 acres are being rapidly made over from these old and unsuitable varieties to the new cross-bred, disease-resistant vines ideal for the growing of wine for domestic consumption.

The white wines of Savoy, Isère and Drôme are better than the reds, nearly always true of mountain wines. In addition to Roussette, already mentioned, there are several other *cépages*: Jacquère, also called Plant des Abymes, yields a white wine with a good bouquet; and Chasselas, here called Fendant, a neutral but quite pleasant and well-balanced wine like some of the best Swiss ones.

So much for the south-eastern vineyard. From Annecy or Aix take the road south to Chambèry, which has a notable 'wine' of its own, an aperitif wine which is in fact a vermouth, that is a fortified and spiced wine into which go certain herbs, usually according to some local and secret recipe.

It has always been a mystery to me why, with so much poor vermouth on the market, Chambèry, in many ways the best of its kind and certainly less 'liverish' than most, is so little known. It used to be possible to get it in some London restaurants, but I have not seen any since the war. At all events, Chambèry being on your way, stop there and try it. Then turn west and drive by way of La Tour du Pin to Lyon.

CHAPTER NINE

THE RHÔNE VALLEY

LYON is a city where I have never 'happened to find myself' for more than a few hours at a time. It is one of those cities which have a very special reputation or notoriety, a 'mystique' of its own. Writers of distinction born in Lyon go elsewhere, write obsessively of their city with a kind of loving hatred, abuse their fellow-townsmen as clods, cold, greedy, deceitful and too shrewd—and return there to settle down in late middle age. When a Parisian or a Marseillais sneers at 'provincialism', he means Lyon. It is the Manchester of France, but in spirit only, for it is not so ugly and it has quite a good climate, although apt to be oppressively humid, and in winter it can be astonishingly cold. It is immensely rich and it has several architectural singularities, notably the arcaded shopping streets, something after the style of the *Galeria* of Milan, but more extensive. It is said that natives of the place who know it really well can get from one end of the city to the other, in any direction, without going into the open air. I confess that the only part of Lyon I know well, because there I spend my time when I pass through, is the enchanting covered food market.

I am aware that this sounds uncommonly greedy, but it is not; my interest and pleasure are what is incorrectly called 'platonic'. The market is a rare and strange place of pleasure for the eye; the stomach does not come into the matter at all. Whoever takes delight in forms and colours can loiter about the clean alleys between the stalls for hours without thinking of the foodstuffs displayed as for eating—at least, until about lunch-time. There is none of the litter of paper and cabbage-leaves and general filth which disgraces so many English markets. The place looks as if it is swept and scrubbed every ten minutes. To gaze on meat butchered by a Lyonnais is not, as elsewhere, to sicken and swear to turn vegetarian, but to admire an artist's handiwork. Many kinds of food ready prepared for cooking are offered, for example, *quenelles*, which involve such a long and tiresome process of pounding in a mortar that even the conscientious housewives of Lyon would hesitate to make them in their own kitchens. Every vegetable offered seems to have been hand-picked for shape and size, and then scrubbed clean and neatly trimmed of leaf and root, like the prize specimens in an important County Horticultural Show, which they resemble. Here, too, one can see why it is that French market-gardeners find it worth their while to produce the finest varieties and go to much trouble in producing super-specimens. English shoppers simply do not distinguish quality in fruit: an apple or pear is an apple or pear. But the French grower can be sure that if he produces Doyenne du Comice pears weighing a pound each and containing a gill of delectable juice, he will get the proper price for them —and not just some arbitrary price covering pears of all kinds, more or less. Here, too, you can see, arranged in neat and attractive patterns for display, the great white Roman snails which the Lyonnais cook so well, ready 'de-slimed' by many days in bran, and carefully starved to the requisite state of leanness.

The Lyon market is, in short, a great gallery of wonderful still-life compositions; and even such puritans as are shocked by the idea of so much care and art being lavished on mere food cannot fail to admire the skill and thoroughness with which it is all done. The others, those who believe with Brillat-Savarin that cooking and eating, among civilized men, should be a minor art, will find in the market the promise for what, come lunch or dinner-time, Lyon has to offer in a hundred restaurants both *classique* and *bourgeois*.

South of Lyon the first, and by far the most important, of the Rhône valley vineyards, is the Côtes-du-Rhône. It is very long indeed, extending from Ampuis in the north to Châteauneuf-du-Pape, a matter of 140 miles. Needless to say, the vineyards are at intervals along this valley and do not fill it. South of Châteauneuf-du-Pape, in the Bouches-du-Rhône, are other vineyards, other Côtes, which we will come to in their turn. The most northerly of the Côtes-du-Rhône are very steep slopes indeed, in fact precipitous; further south the vines are found on gentler slopes or even on the flat. All these Côtes produce white, red and *rosé* wines, high in alcohol, full-bodied, generous, and surprising in their great diversity.

First an outline of the geography of the Côtes. About eight miles south of Vienne, on the Rhône, there are two important vineyards on opposite banks: Côte Rôtie on the west, Condrieux on the east. Three miles farther south, on the west bank, is Château Grillet. Fifty kilometres of valley road farther south again—the road runs parallel with the river—is the Hermitage vineyard, the most distinguished of the whole Côtes, the nearest towns being Tain l'Hermitage on the east bank, and Tournon on the west. Twenty miles farther south you come to Valence, which is more on the east bank than the west, but straddles the river. A mile or two north-west of it are the Cornas and St. Peray vineyards. That completes the northern half of the wine Côtes.

There are lesser vineyards in the next eighty-odd miles of southerly driving, but none of importance until you come to Châteauneuf-du-Pape, south of the very attractive town of Orange, of which more anon. North-east of Châteauneuf-du-Pape, through Beaumes-de-Venise, is another vineyard, the Côtes du Ventoux; and south of those Côtes, nearly on the Durance, the Côtes de Luberon.

The centre for the southern Côtes is Avignon, or Orange if you prefer a smaller town; for the northern ones, Valence. Nobody but a person on very urgent business, or a lunatic, would, however, drive straight down the valley from the latter to the former; I shall explain why in a moment, but briefly it is clearly a piece pushed out of Dante's Hell as too unpleasant for any self-respecting Inferno. The soil of this long and narrow wine country varies from granitic in the north, through red earth alluviums as you work southwards to the silica sands of the Tavel vineyard near Châteauneuf-du-Pape. As for the *cépages*, there are many more of these authorized than in the case of any other *Appellation d'Origine*, although there are perhaps more names than really distinct varieties. Even though difference in name does signify some small difference in kind, the vines of the Rhône can be grouped in similar varieties—types, as it were: these are Syrah, Viognier, Roussanne and Marsanne, as the most important of the *cépages* groups peculiar to the region. But many which we are familiar with from other viticultural provinces are also planted.

As I have already hinted, motoring down the arterial road from Valence to Avignon, or for that matter from Lyon to the Bouches-du-Rhône, is not a pleasant experience. It is one of the nastiest examples I know of the new type of main-road urbanism, the long sprawl of ugliness, noise, stench, ill-temper, bad and expensive hotels and restaurants and pull-ups, eye-sores, architectural blains and festers, which extends from San Francisco to Budapest, and for all I know to Pekin; from Edinburgh to Casablanca. It has neither nationality nor character, its jargons and *lingua franca* are mutilated speech, it is a physical symbol of the expense of spirit in a waste of shame. It is the monument of the twentieth century. In the case of that section of it in question here, it is made much worse than elsewhere by the fact that the French, in all other respects the most civilized of peoples, go barking mad at the wheel of a car or truck. It is not so much that they are bad drivers, as that they are savagely ill-tempered drivers. I do not pretend to explain this, I merely observe that it is so. The Spaniards, it is true, are viciously selfish on the road, but Spain is fortunately too poor to have many cars. The Italians drive flat-out in all conditions, and pass on blind corners; but they are in the first place ten times as alert and twice as skilful as we are; and in addition they are cheerful and good-mannered about it. It must be admitted that English driving is exasperating to the Latin: it is slow, clumsy, obstinate. But the French . . !

The point is, the visitor to the Rhône vineyards can avoid a bad section of this infamous N7 by making detours which will take him off it at Valence and again at Orange and bring him back to it at Avignon, and take him through some very beautiful hill-country which is quiet and clean and tranquil. It is also possible to avoid the northern section, after Condrieux, by going through Annonay, Yssingeaux and Lamastre, returning to N7 at Valence, which takes you over the Monts du Vivarais by a number of beautiful and quite alarming, though not very high, mountain passes. Then, after you have done with the Valence region, turn west to Grenoble, thence go south through the lovely country of the Drac valley and over the Col de la Haute Croix to Aspres-sur-Buech. There, take the south-westerly valley to pick up the river Eygues at Nyons, which will bring you back to the main road at Bourg St. Andrea about sixteen kilometres north of Orange. These are, it is true, long detours. But they are worth while for their own sake, you will see something of France and of Provence, which you certainly will not if you stick to the subtopian horror of the main road to the Riviera—the sight, sound and stench of which is enough to ruin any holiday.

As I have said, perhaps too often and too loudly, N7 is, barring a few details, indistinguishable from our own Great West, or the trunk roads of the United States, or the *autobahnen*, or an Italian *autostrada*. If you like to see people who still have some characteristic style; if you like to stay in quiet and decent inns and eat wholesome food at reasonable prices, you must avoid the great roads. And in Provence it is particularly well worth while to do this, because the province and its people are nothing like the image of them which bad art and bad literature and sloppy thinking have created, and which both have, in some measure, come to resemble in the more popular, frequented parts, where it is expected of them, and where it is commercially advisable to be like the tourist-trade advertisements, rather than like life.

Parts, rare parts, of Provence are lush: with that lushness goes a certain easiness of temper, a certain relaxation of spirit. This, idealized and falsified, has been made to represent the province as a whole, just as, for example, the melancholy, secret, humourless character of the Irish has come to be misrepresented by what one might call *Begorrahism*. But characteristic Provence has for long, very long, been savaged by the pitiless sun, scourged by the cruel *mistral,* worn to the bone. You will not find there, if you look a little way below the surface, the laughing, easygoing people of the journalistic imagination and the railway poster. Why on earth should you? These people live a hard, a grim life, the sun their enemy, the wind their enemy, the soil lean and ungrateful. Stand and stare up at the *palais des Papes* at Avignon, and consider the spirit of the land that made that grim building which, because it happens to shine whitely, does not immediately strike one as grim; for grim and grey go together in the northern imagination.

A good deal of the rubbish which has become the popular idea of Provence is due to that unscrupulous sentimentalist Alphonse Daudet, a man of great talent but no artistic insight . . . or little integrity—I do not know which. Unlike that other, and toweringly greater, regionalist among French writers, de Maupassant, whose Norman peasants are drawn with a stark truth not easy to 'take', Daudet, in Provence, and excepting in odd moments when he wrote some penetrating short pieces, rejected reality and invented Provencaux of his own. Lesser artists have followed suit. What is to some extent justified in Daudet by charm, is justified in the later artists by nothing; for they only had to go and look and listen to find out that they were writing about a cloud-cuckoo land.

The hard, lean men and dark-eyed, sullen women of this land are about as jolly and laughing as desert Arabs, whom they sometimes resemble. Nor should the pretty Arlesienne caps and Nîmois aprons be allowed to fool you. Are these the people who so revel in sensuality, in wine, women and song, who laugh and play and shrug off the serious things in life? If you are misled into thinking so, remember what part of all Europe it was which alone adopted, and with fanaticism, the fiercely life-denying, life-hating creed of the Manichee and for its sake denied themselves the ordinary, natural outlet of physical love, rejected the flesh as no people, not the most dour of northern Calvinists, have ever done before or since, and sought death gladly, even the young children. It was in Provence that the ferocious Catholic crusade, led by the ruthless Simon de Montfort, was required to stamp out a heresy which was a flat denial of life at its very sources.

Certainly the Provençaux have another side: not all is false in Daudet. The holiday-maker with no time or inclination to penetrate the surface will encounter the easier, pleasanter, smiling face of the people, the face which goes with their warm and generous wine. But unless he gets off that appalling main road, which perhaps proves that the Manichean force of darkness, so feared by the people of Provence that they denied the flesh, did at last prevail in Provence, he will not see any real people at all.

Côte Rôtie

The *premiers crus* of the first great vineyard south of Vienne are entitled to the *Appellation* Côte Rôtie: they are grown on the very steep slopes where the river passes through what is almost a gorge. The permitted *cépages* are two, Viognier and Syrah (*syn.* Serine). These wines are red and they must have an alcohol content of at least 10°, but as a rule they have more. They are wines of great distinction and delicious fragrance, justifying the poetic images which the more uninhibited writers on wine sometimes apply to them. Next, going southward, are the Condrieux wines, made only from the Viognier grape and with an alcohol minimum of 11°. These do not differ markedly from the Côte Rôtie wines and can easily be confused with them. This applies, but much less so, to the white wines of the third north Rhône *Appellation*, Château Grillet. None of these three great wines is well known by name to English wine-drinkers, but the fourth in geographical order is very well known, and deserves to be, for Hermitage ranks among the greatest wines in the world and a fine vintage can safely be set beside even the noblest Burgundies.

The *cépages* of Hermitage are three: Syrah, Roussanne and Marsanne. Both the red and the white must have not less than 10° alcohol, though they usually have rather more than that; and there is also a Hermitage straw wine which has to have 14°.

As one would expect in the case of wines grown in the heat of the Côte Rôtie—or of any of the côtes down to

Hermitage—all the wines of this region, but notably the reds, improve with age. They are kept for three years or longer in the wood; and the best of them should be kept for at least another seven years in bottle before being drunk. Ten years in bottle will not hurt them; but, in so far as any such rule is possible, fifteen years is too long. At something between ten and twelve years of age, then, the wines of the Côte Rôtie, of Condrieux, Château Grillet and Hermitage, develop their distinctive bouquet and flavour and body, and acquire the perfect balance for which the careful mixture of *cépages*, and the climate of their selected vineyard sites, are responsible. The fact that the reputation of these wines, especially the three northern ones, is not greater than it is, is at least partly due to their being commonly drunk too young, when they are relatively harsh.

The named vineyards of the Côtie Rôtie are nine: La Garenne, Le Grand Clos, Le Moulin, Pommiere et Turque, La Landonne, La Grande Plantée, La Grosse-Roche, Tharamon-de-Gron and Pavillon Rouge. There are three named Condrieux wines, Condrieu, Verin and St. Michel. As for Château Grillet, it is one of those wines which is more talked about and written about than sampled: one of the most distinguished of the world's white wines, it all comes from a single four-acre vineyard, and the chances of finding it on a wine-list outside Lyon or Vienne are remote.

Hermitage

The great red wines of Hermitage are all from the Syrah grape, and if you want to test their real quality and have the palate to do so, you must insist on a wine not less than eight years old. The Hermitage whites are rarely as good as Château Grillet, but easier to come by and give some idea of its quality. As for the straws, the yellows, it is for them that the Roussanne and Marsanne grapes are cultivated, and they should be drunk not only as to age but as to the food you eat with them, as if they were red wines. They are dry, substantial and to be treated with respect; they cannot be recommended to people whose livers are less robust than they might be.

*   *   *   *   *   *

I have said nothing about the history of these vineyards because, unlike the other French vineyards, their story belongs not with the wine-history of France but with the wine-history of the Roman Empire. South of Vienne, vineyards are apt to be older than French civilization, and their beginning may be found as far back as the foundation of the Phocian colony of Marseille. It was almost certainly from that province that the vine spread northwards as far as Vienne well before the Romans had economic and political control of the whole Rhône valley. In other words, the origins of the Rhône wines are more or less taken for granted and not given special attention by historians or local chroniclers, although Pliny has interesting things to say about the varieties of the vine grown and the kind of wine they yielded. Naturally, there are early medieval legends about the origins of the Rhône vineyards, but they are all glaringly self-conscious, in fact bogus, like the one concerning the origin of the Hermitage wines: this says that wine-growers were sent by heaven to quench the thirst of the holy hermit whose cave can still be visited, and from which the vineyards take their name. This tale has only one merit. By implying, as it does, that a man living within walking distance of a large river was suffering from thirst, it makes it quite clear that water should not be regarded as a drink fit for human consumption. This is sound. I was once told by that great but eccentric specialist in longevity, Dr. Julien Besançon that wine, not water, should be regarded as the natural drink of man, and that water was a dangerous poison. I was pleased, but surprised, and pointed out that water was what all animals on earth normally drink. To this the doctor replied, 'Yes, and they die of it', and pointed out that man was the smallest consumer of water among the mammals of comparable size, and the longest lived of them all. Beer, he said, was at least better than water, tea or coffee, all of which he condemned as most unwholesome. Nor did he approve of spirits, excepting perhaps a mouthful of very good brandy after a meal.

However, whether the tale be bogus or not, the hermit's shrine is worth a visit, not for its own sake, for it is devoid of interest, but for the view which its site affords over the vineyards and the river itself. Among them some of the following Hermitage vineyards are visible:

Vineyards on the granite slopes, producing red wines:
Les Hermitages
Sizeranne
Rochefine
Marquise de la Tourette

Vineyards on the limestone slopes producing white wines:
Chante-Alouette
Maison Blanche
Mure de Larnage

Vineyards producing whites and reds regardless of subsoil:
Cuvée de Gallier
La Chapelle
Belleroche

In addition to these 'first growth' wines, the region produces, in the four *départements* of Rhône, Loire, Ardeche and Drôme, lesser but still excellent wines bearing the names of their *communes* of origin and which, if they attain 1° of alcohol in excess of the legal minimum, are entitled to add the words *Côtes du Rhône* to the bottle label.

The visitor to all the vineyards mentioned above, and also to Crozes-Hermitage in the Drôme, can choose either Tain l'Hermitage or Tournon as a centre, although both are on the main road which runs, in all its frightfulness, on both sides of the river, so that both towns are noisy and more or less expensive. Valence is preferable for the next three vineyards farther south; after that it is best to make the detour already suggested and to see something of the country where it has not yet been internationalized and hideously corrupted.

The three vineyards near Valence are Cornas, St. Joseph and St. Peray, in the Ardèche *département*. Their slopes are not quite so steep, for the Rhône valley begins to open out. Cornas grows only the Syrah grape and makes only red wine, minimum 11°, in a number of named vineyards. The wines are full and heavy and need about eight years in bottle, but do not, for a reason I have never understood, keep for much longer. For my part, indeed, I do not care for these wines, they seem to me to be inferior versions of the red Hermitages—they are cheaper too, of course—so that they have, as it were, not much point. The same applies to the red St. Joseph wines; they are wanting in character and distinction. The St. Joseph whites, on the other hand, when about ten years of age, seem to me quite as good as the white Hermitages—in short, excellent.

St. Peray grows Roussanne and Marsanne, the vines planted for the yellow Hermitage, but in this case yielding a natural white wine of about 11° which is very good indeed; and a sparkling white wine which has been known to connoisseurs of 'champagne' in France since the last century but which has never, as far as I can discover, penetrated to England. The still whites of St. Peray have an ancient reputation, for they are among those cited by Pliny in the chapter of his work already quoted. The sparkling whites are all right for those who like bubbles in their wine; in fact I am told that they are superb; for my taste they are a waste of good grapes.

Châteauneuf-du-Pape

It might perhaps be true to say that Châteauneuf-du-Pape is the most southerly vineyard in Europe to produce a great wine of real delicacy and subtlety at a low altitude. It is set at about 100 feet above sea-level in the blazing plain of the Bouches-du-Rhône—far too hot a site, one might have thought, to produce a wine of such character and refinement. Let me make myself clear; all natural wines, correctly grown and vinted, and which nobody has mucked about with, are good. But wines of the deep south, where temperatures are very high and sunshine excessive, are not subtle, not 'interesting'. They are simply sound and strong. Typical are some of the harsh, thick red wines of Tuscany, and the nameless wine of Languedoc. It is true that Italy and Spain produce some fine, delicate wines, as well as just wine; but they are always grown at relatively high altitudes. Soave, that delicious north Italian white wine, is grown well to the north of Châteauneuf-du-Pape and at something like 1,500 feet above sea-level. Rioja, the best of the natural

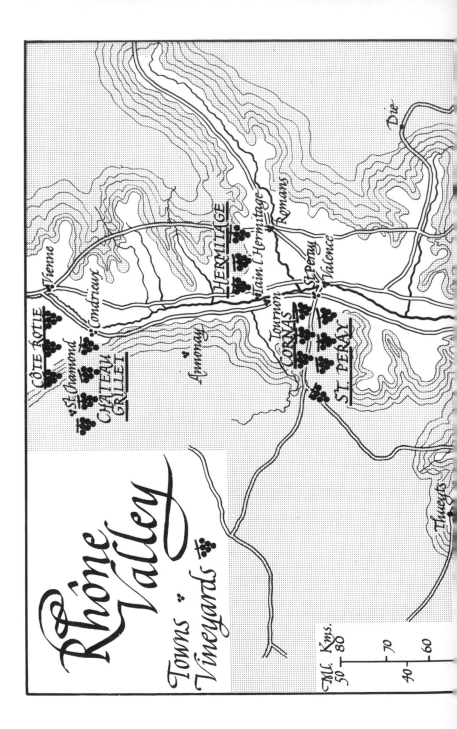

Rhône Valley

Towns :: Vineyards 🍇

M. Kms.
50 — 80
70
40
60

Vienne
Côte Rôtie
St. Diamond
Château Grillet
Condrieux
Annonay
Hermitage
Crozin l'Hermitage
Romans
Tournon
Cornas
St. Peray
Valence
St. Peray
Die
Thueyts

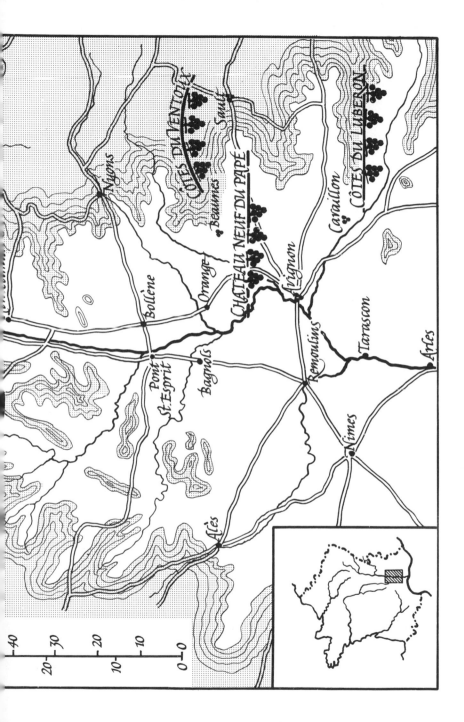

CÔTES DU VENTOUX

Suzette

Beaumes

Nyons

CHÂTEAU NEUF DU PAPE

Cavaillon

CÔTES DU LUBERON

Orange

Bollène

Avignon

Pont St.-Esprit

Bagnols

Remoulins

Tarascon

Arles

Alès

Nîmes

20
10
0

40
30
20
10
0

wines of Spain, is a mountain wine. Frascati, the most delicate of the Roman wines, is grown about two degrees of latitude south of Châteauneuf-du-Pape; but at about a thousand feet of altitude. So that, as it seems to me, the undeniable quality of Châteauneuf-du-Pape is a very remarkable achievement.

North of this famous vineyard lies Orange, one of the most attractive towns in Provence, the terrific heat of its summers so mitigated by the dense shade of enormous and ancient plane trees that the fountain in the square is deliciously cool even in a heat wave, with perpetually damp beards of moss and lichen hanging from its basin. I think it is the only town in the province where I have never seen the plane trees, so vital to comfort in that sweltering valley, ruined by pollarding.

The whole countryside south from Orange, through Avignon and Arles to Aigues-Mortes and the Camargue, is strange, melancholy, oppressive, fascinating. As you approach it you forget all you have ever read about sun-baked Provence being gay. God knows there is nothing merry about the stony, windy waste of the Crau; about the seething, teeming marsh of the Camargue, with its herds of bulls, its hard-faced mounted herdsmen, and the sad loveliness of its sudden flights of flamingoes; nor about the frightening, grim city of Aigues Mortes or the white and noisy glare of Arles. None of this is quite European; it is a sort of displaced Africa, with a history of religious madness, ruthless war, and the strangest kind of love ever invented, the love which was the inspiration of the troubadours, which they had from an Arab source—or at least their songs were of Arab origin. As for their love, it was a case of much cry and little wool, a love which issued in despair, devotion and a chastity which was perverse.

This is the country which nevertheless produces some of the best wine in the world, the wine of the southern Côtes-du-Rhône: the three major *crus* are:

In the *département* of the Vaucluse:

Châteauneuf-du-Pape. These are exceptional wines in that no less than thirteen *cépages* are authorized in their making. They may be red, white or *rosé*, but the most famous wine of this name is, of course, the red. Whatever the colour, the alcohol minimum has to be 12·5° and it is usually more.

In the *département* of the Gard:

Tavel. There are seven authorized *cépages*. The wine is *rosé*, actually nearer to orange than pink, and it has to be 11° alcohol or more. It is one of the very few wines I personally dislike, for, in my opinion, it is 'quarrelsome'. A *rosé* should, I believe, be lighter.

Lirac. There are eleven authorized varieties grown. The wines are red, white or *rosé* and the minimum degree is 11·5.

As in the case of the north Rhône vineyard, there are also a number of other wines in this part of the region which are entitled to call themselves Côtes-du-Rhône, added to the name of the *commune*, on the label. They are, in the Vaucluse, Gigondas and Caironne; in the Gard, Landin and Chusclan. These wines are of similar character to the named Côtes-du-Rhône wines, that is to say they are very substantial and high in alcohol, but without the distinction of a good Châteauneuf-du-Pape.

The quantities of Châteauneuf-du-Pape, Tavel and Lirac produced every year are relatively very small. Suitably lean and stony soils are plentiful enough, but the vineyards have never been restored to their former extent after being more or less wiped out by *Phylloxera* late in the last century. Châteauneuf-du-Pape itself—it is named after an old summer palace of the Popes used during the long Vatican schism when there were Popes and anti-Popes, and now a ruin—has been restored to oenological respectability only during the last quarter of a century or thereabouts, for the original re-planting after the *Phylloxera* disaster was done with American vines and some of the first and worst hybrids, so that the wine was of inferior quality. In making a great to-do about restoring the original thirteen traditional *cépages* of the re-gion, the south Rhône growers have chosen small output and specific high quality, vesting their interest in a rela-tively expensive wine. No doubt this was wise, for the alter-native was to compete with Languedoc and Algeria in the production of cheap *vin courant*, the price of which is apt to suffer grievously in years of high production. Besides, such is our peculiar civilization that it is probably safer to be selling a luxury to the rich than a necessity to the poor !

In both the Vaucluse and the Gard the practice of 'mulching' the vineyards with large stones is quite common, especially in the better-managed vineyards. It is an ancient practice, and has a dual purpose: the stones absorb heat during the day and give it out at night, thus maintaining a relatively high temperature among the ripening grapes at night time; and they keep the soil beneath them moist by preventing evaporation of soil water. This usage entails difficulties in cultivation, of course, as the stones wear out cultivating tools very quickly. The practice arose, at least in this part of the world, quite naturally from the fact that the soil is in any case very stony indeed; in fact, where it is required to cultivate crops other than vines, a preliminary clearance of stones is necessary, for although cereal and other crops also benefit from a mulch of stones, the wear and tear of machinery and tools—not to mention tempers— would be excessive.

Orange, in addition to the amenities already mentioned, has, like Nîmes and Arles, a Roman amphitheatre rather large for a provincial town, since it will hold 10,000 people. Provence was, of course, the oldest Gallic province of the Roman empire (hence its name), and was Hellenized long before the conquest, a fact which is constantly apparent in its buildings—the arena at Orange, the Maison Carée at Nîmes, the famous aqueduct called the Pont du Gard, one of the most moving of ancient buildings—presumably because of its dramatic appearance, magnificent setting and social significance. As in Arles, the amphitheatre is still in use at Orange, principally for the annual drama festival in late July, where some of the best companies in France are usually to be seen, including that of the *Comédie Française*. Since Roman engineers, copying their Greek mentors, had long mastered the art of acoustics, the Orange open-air theatre is the best I have ever visited.

Another use for the Roman arenas of Provence is bull-fighting, very appropriate to the climate of Provence and to the tragic nature of its people. There are no good

French or, as far I know, Provençal bull-fighters, so that one of these spectacles is worth seeing only if, as is quite usual, one or two of the best Spanish matadors have been engaged. For bull-fighting is rather like the little girl in the nursery rhyme, when it is good it is very, very good, but when it is bad it is . . . downright revolting. Only a matador who is a fine artist can make us forget the brutal cruelty of the spectacle in the beauty and excitement of this ballet in which Death is the principal dancer.

* * * * * *

We have not yet exhausted the Côtes-du-Rhône wines. If you drive out of Orange on a side road numbered D69, towards Vaison-la-Romaine, where the Roman forum is still in being and has no more to recommend it than a standardized provincial town-hall of our own epoch (Roman building rarely has anything but sheer ponderous endurance), you will find yourself at Rastau. There they cultivate a vine called Grenache, widely planted throughout the south Rhône region in general, and from which is made a naturally sweet wine with the official *Appellation* Rastau. Sample it after a meal, or with fresh fruit, then turn south and drive—it is all interesting, burnt, bony country, growing greener and fresher as you climb—to Beaumes-de-Venise. There the vine is one of the numerous Muscats, and the wine a heavy, syrupy, musky dessert wine called Muscat de Beaume-de-Venise. Since it is not fortified it is probably more wholesome than either port or sherry, but it is still rather liverish stuff.

West of Beaumes-de-Venise is another hill vineyard, not really a part of the Rhône group at all, and with its own *Appellation,* Côtes-de-Ventoux. It is, however, planted to the typical Rhône *cépages*—Grenache, Syrah, Mourvedre, Roussanne, Ugni blanc and some others. The best wine of these slopes is VDQS. The same applies to the wine of the Côtes-de-Luberon, south of Ventoux and just north of the Durance valley. Both of these are hill wines and lighter than Côtes-du-Rhône. From the Côtes-de-Luberon, supposing you have made this second easterly detour from the main road, you can return to it at Avignon, going by way of Apt.

Avignon: yes, well, it is a matter of taste. Certainly the great *palais des Papes*, towering above the Rhône valley, should be visited and its tremendous view enjoyed. There is, too, the famous pont d'Avignon, sticking only half-way across the stream, where,

> L'on y danse,
> l'on y chante . . .

The city, like the countryside, is glaring, dusty, noisy, harsh. It would be more impressive if the huddle of squalid, petty commerce were to be cleared away from the walls. Yet in that case it would cease to live and become, like Carcassonne, a colossal museum-piece. With both Orange and Tarascon within easy reach, I would not, I think, recommend staying at Avignon.

Of all the Provençal towns Tarascon comes nearest to confirming the Daudet idea of that country, a quiet, well-shaded, dreaming, good-natured place—at least on the surface. Yet for my part I have wondered whether Daudet's Tartarin de Tarascon, a comic character as well loved in French literature as Sam Weller in English, was really a foreigner, determined to be more Provençal that the Provençaux as he saw them, as we all tend to see them, and as they are not. Tartarin, it will be remembered, was a principal in the extraordinary game played by the Tarasconais, the game of shooting their own caps—by way of clay pigeons—during their Saturday or Sunday afternoon outings, their passion for *la chasse* having exterminated the game, and even the song-birds, of the entire region. That part, at least, is true enough.

I shall not forget my own visit, some years ago now, to the famous mill where Daudet wrote those *Lettres de mon moulin* and that whimsical *La Mule du Pape* which are inflicted upon Advanced French students. That visit provided a sharp lesson for such authors as count upon posthumous respect as prophets even in their own country, albeit adopted. The mill is now a literary shrine, and I had a long talk with its *gardien*. He knew nothing and cared less about Alphonse Daudet, beyond what his official position required of him; he recited his piece about the great author, but parrot-fashion. But he turned out to be beyond comparison the most interesting expert on Charles Dickens that I have ever talked to.

Before leaving the Rhône valley vineyards—in addition to *Appellation* wines, Côtes-du-Rhône, *communes* of the Côtes-du-Rhône, VDQS of Ventoux and Luberon, *grands crus* of Hermitage, Châteauneuf-du-Pape, Lirac, Tavel, and the rest, the valley produces a great deal of *vin de consommation courante,* what one might properly call daily wine on the analogy of daily bread. Some of this is made from grapes of the traditional local *cépages,* but more and more from PD vines, notably Coudercs, Seibels and Seyve-Villards of diverse numbers. It is excellent picnic wine with which to fill your bottle from the wood. The three principal southern wine *départements* of the valley, Ardèche, Drôme and Vaucluse, have 100,000 wine-growing smallholders cultivating 175,000 acres of vines producing approximately 50 million gallons of wine per annum.

There is, in short, no need at all to drink water in Provence.

CHAPTER TEN

THE VINEYARDS OF THE MIDI

For viticultural and oenological purposes the *midi* of France, unlike 'all Gaul', is divided into four parts. The word *midi* is here used, by the way, to mean only the 'deep south'. Here are the divisions:

1. *The Provençal Vineyard*

This is included within the *départements* of *Alpes Maritimes, Var, Bouches-du-Rhône, Basses-Alpes* and, if the upper reaches of the river Durance be counted as Provence, *Hautes-Alpes*. With the exception of the Bouches-du-Rhône and a small piece of the Var, all this is magnificent mountain country of exciting roads, attractive and very diverse towns, strange mountain villages—sometimes with their ancient fortifications intact—torrential streams, waterfalls and gorges, abounding in spring flowers. Its coast, fashionable still, crowded and ruinously expensive, is probably best avoided excepting for an occasional raid to visit a market, and get some swimming if you can find a beach which is not monopolized by some hut-letting racketeer, and to eat sea-food.

2. *The Corsican Vineyard*

This is of small extent, about 16,000 acres under vines, and interesting only as a curiosity. Frenchmen drink Corsican wine both as an aperitif and as a dessert wine. If the vineyards are insignificant, however, the island, as a holiday resort, is far from it. In May and early June it is a place of enchantment.

3. *The Languedoc Vineyard*

Languedoc is the plain and foothills country south-east of the Cevennes mountains, and like them sweeping in an arc from about Carcassonne to about Tournon on the Rhône, although these ancient provinces can no longer be very exactly defined excepting historically. For the benefit of those who do not know the fact already, Languedoc is Langue d'Oc. In the early middle ages France had two languages, the Langue d'Oc and the Langue d'Oil. The former survives as Provençal . . . the whole of Provence was, of course, a separate kingdom and not part of what we now know as France. The Langue d'Oil developed into French proper.

The Languedoc vineyard is within the *départements* of *Gard, Hérault* and *Aude*. The plantations of vines are enormous and for the most part they produce ordinary wine for everyday consumption, in vast bulk. The vinification is industrialized, with concrete vats holding up to quarter of a million gallons, and fully mechanized. The area of these vineyards of the plains extends from somewhere near Carcassonne to north of Nîmes, and from the Cevennes foothills to the Gulf of the Lion. This gulf I shall always remember, if only because it deposited a full plate of soup, two open bottles of wine, an oil and vinegar set, and a cruet of salt and pepper in my lap—I was wearing a brand-new gabardine suit—as I was sailing for Corsica on an apparently perfectly calm day. It has, in fact, a reputation rather like the Bay of Biscay—that is, it can be remarkably rough. On the whole, however, it is tranquil enough excepting 'crossing the bar'. As for the other boundary of the Languedoc vineyards, the Cevennes, it was there that I discovered one of the most beautiful of the great *pulsatilla* anemones (though the botanists have decided we are no longer to call them anemones), growing wild.

4. *The Rousillon Vineyard*

The *département* is *Pyrénées-Orientales*. Perpignan is the principal town and the centre of the vineyards of the plain, which are of economic but no oenological importance. The important wines here are all sweet, fortified dessert wines.

The country is bounded on the east by the Gulf of the Lion, on the west by the Republic of Andorra and on the south by Spanish Catalonia.

I will deal with 1, 3 and 4 in this chapter, and devote a short chapter to Corsica alone.

PROVENCE

Concerning the nature of this province, I have already said what I have to say, because at the southern end of the Rhône vineyard we were already in Provence. But considered as an oenological province it includes not only the characteristic harshness of the Bouches-du-Rhône plains, marshes, wastes and strange cities, but also a very different kind of country, the maritime Alps behind the once ultra-fashionable and still smart Riviera coast. Although grapes for the table, and also for wine, are grown in these mountains, the important viticultural regions lie elsewhere.

THE CAMARGUE

In the east is the plain vineyard of the Camargue. It produces fairly strong, fairly full-bodied red wine of the same sound, ordinary kind as 'Algerian' and its principal use is for blending with red wines of more character in other parts of the south. As a simple daily wine, drawn from the wood to fill your picnic bottle, it is very adequate.

The nearest large town for the Camargue, which is one of the most fascinating pieces of country in Europe for the holiday-maker of unconventional tastes, is Arles. It has much to recommend it, being animated, prosperous, full of interesting antiquities and memories of Van Gogh, and at the same time equipped with a number of very good hotels, notably the Nord-Pinus and the Jules César, at both of which I have stayed in much comfort. On the other hand it is abominably noisy, hot and dusty in summer and autumn, so that the place I would choose to stay at, right in the Camargue, small, relatively quiet and on the sea, is Les-Saintes-Maries-de-la-Mer, the Holy-Marys-of-the-Sea. The name derives from a legend concerning the Three Marys, said to have been cast ashore and settled there, after the Resurrection. The town's only architectural distinction is King

René's (King of Provence) ninth-century church. Its crypt contains a shrine which is of particular holiness in the eyes of Europe's gipsy population. Once a year gipsies from all over the continent congregate there in thousands, coming in every kind of conveyance from painted waggons to plated Cadillacs for an annual religious festival which, if it be more or less Catholic now, has certainly not always been so. For the origins of this ceremony probably go back beyond Christianity.

The Camargue is a vast expanse of salt-marsh, prairie, bog, lagoon and beaches. Its flora is peculiar, copious and diverse: among other things, I have gathered excellent wild asparagus there, and at one time there were people who gathered it for market. The place is also a paradise for bird-watchers, the most spectacular species being the flamingoes, but there are scores of others both native and migrant, water-fowl, waders, song-birds and hawks. Parts are under cultivation: there, as well as vines, are maize, cotton, even some rice. On the prairies of short, salt pastures or long tough grass and weeds, roam the herds of Camargue fighting bulls, bred for the ring, peaceful and unaggressive beasts when herded together and at ease in their natural environment, but fierce and warlike when cut out from the herd and set face to face with an enemy. It is possible that the Camargue may be one of the immemorial habitats, possibly the original one, of the European wild cattle. At least, these bulls are said to have primitive traits which makes it possible that their kind is one of the sources of our scores of modern breeds. The tranquil herds, grazing in freedom, virtually wild, are cared for by a body of 'cowboys', the *gardiens de la Camargue*, men picturesquely dressed and living their lives on horseback. In mid-summer the whole region is sometimes fragrant with the scent of herbs, for the dry parts produce all the aromatics as part of the natural flora, lavender and thyme, rue and pungent kinds of mint.

Such are the surroundings of the Camargue vineyards, a strange and exciting land for those who like walking, pottering, botanizing, watching plants and birds, communing with themselves and nature in a brooding, sultry mood, rather than with crowds of their own kind.

The vineyards themselves are extensive, large properties in few hands; and, which is extremely rare nowadays, the vines are not grafted but grown on their own roots; for the Camargue vine-growers' practice is to flood the vineyards for several weeks in each year and with water which is apt to be brackish. In such conditions the root-dwelling *Phylloxera* aphis cannot survive, and the vines, although rather short-lived, yield colossal crops. The only other places in Europe where similar practices, because similar conditions, obtain, is the mouth of the river Po, which is also incidentally the only other European place frequented by flamingoes.

The varieties of vine grown are numerous, but much less so than formerly. The most important, in point of numbers, is Carignan for red wine and Ugni blanc for white. For quality, Aramon is probably the principal vine. There are also plantations of the ancient Clairette vine, various *teinturiers* to give a rich colour to the red wine, and an increasing number of PD vines. The same varieties are to be found throughout the plain vineyards of the Languedoc.

To the east of the Camargue is a vineyard region producing wines of rather more distinction. This is a shallow arc of land along the lower slopes of the Maures range of hills, and it is known, for oenological purposes, as the *Côtes-de-Provence*. These Côtes extend from north of Cassis (which lies east of Marseilles) to Fréjus, the naval base on the inlet whose mouth has St. Raphael on one side and Ste. Maxine on the other. Thus the coast which lies south-east of the Côtes-de-Provence is about half of the most famous piece of seaside in the world, including such holiday resorts as Hyères, La Cavalière, St. Tropez, and others. Of this it is not necessary to write a word, for it has been written about *ad nauseam*. Of course it is a beautiful coast; of course it has a wonderful climate. Equally, of course, it is far too crowded and extortionately expensive. And there are too many filling-stations!

The Côtes-de-Provence produce, in general, VDQS wines of which some *crus classés*—selected growths—are superior to the generality, though rarely to be found outside the hotels and restaurants of the Côte d'Azur, for the quantities produced are small. These classified growths come from small, strictly limited vineyards of the Côtes, most of them in the Bouches-du-Rhône *département* on the west of the Côtes, or in the Var, but one in the Alpes-Maritimes at the eastern end of the Maures foothills.

Some of these named wines are very good indeed. Bandol, from the small Var vineyard about the town of that name, is one such. Production is only 200,000 bottles a year, however. Cassis is another wine of the same kind, and again in such short supply that exporting it is not possible. Better still, if you can get some, is Palette, from a tiny vineyard at the Bouches-du-Rhône end of the Côtes.

East of the Côtes-du-Rhône is the lowest and best of the Alpes-Maritimes vineyards, Bellet, in the *commune* of Nice, which gives its name to a wine with its own *Appellation* and a production of about 5,000 bottles a year, so that it is hardly possible to taste the wine beyond Nice itself. It is not the only Alpes-Maritimes wine, but it is the only one of distinction.

All Provençal wines, excepting the very best, are robust rather than delicate, substantial and strong rather than subtle. But then Provençal food is so highly spiced, so rich in strong flavours, that a robust wine is required to stand up to it. Thus the local wines are perfectly appropriate to the local food.

The Alpes-Maritimes *département*, viticulturally the least important of the wine-provinces of France, is touristically the most important; for its holiday amenities are beyond comparison the most obviously attractive in Europe. The fact that I personally tend to avoid this coast does not, of course, mean anything except to me—most people consider it a sort of paradise.

Of its coast nothing need be said beyond pointing out that it includes the great Sybaris towns of Cannes, Nice and Monte-Carlo, and the smaller but not less famous ones of St. Juan-les-Pins, Antibes and Mentone. But the mountains behind this coast, although one or two places in them have become and to some extent remain fashionable, are much less well known. And since, at least for the motorist, there is no serious inconvenience in being ten or twenty, or even more, miles from the coast and the daily sea and sun bathe, it is no bad idea to stay well back from the crowd and expense of the seaside, and enjoy the combination of warmth and sunshine with mountain freshness and greenness—and lower prices—afforded by the maritime Alpine towns.

Best known of the larger ones is Grasse, a white and hilly town of no architectural graces, but pleasant enough, and famous for its scent manufactories. Although a great deal of scent is now synthetic, the essential oils of flowers are still used for the better kinds, so that quite an important rural industry throughout the Alpes-Maritimes is growing flowers for the Grasse *parfumeries*. The trade is important without being primary. The orange trees, cultivated on south-facing terraces quite high in the mountains, yield two crops, the most important being the flowers, picked for scent, and which make some of the long, narrow valleys below Vence fragrant; thereafter, the fruit, developing from such flowers as are left on the trees. Here and there in the mountains, where the soil is lean and dry over the rock, you come upon vast, symmetrically planted fields of lavender which are given a singularly formal air by the fact that each plant in the long grey-green rows grows into a neat dome of foliage and does not, as in Britain, become leggy with age, partly because the plants are constantly picked back, and partly because they are starved of water, for the rainfall is very low. As evidence that much modern scent is chemically compounded, and not extracted from the flowers, lavender plantations are often neglected and going back to the original mountain scrub.

Grasse also provides a secondary market for the very numerous smallholders who grow flowers for the florists. The small farmers of these mountains, formerly subsistence peasants, are now, to a dangerous extent, dependent upon the luxury trade of the coast for their living. Some grow fruit—grapes and peaches for example, and figs—for the coastal towns. Others grow nothing but flowers, the most important being roses and carnations. In both cases, blooms of certain varieties rejected as not perfect enough for the flower-market at Nice—which is perhaps the greatest of its kind in the world and an unforgettable spectacle—can be sent to the Grasse factories. (Which, by the way, can be visited; all have a staff of guides to show visitors round.)

Not by any means all the vast quantity of flowers grown in the Alpes-Maritimes is absorbed by the local market: roses and carnations, violets and mimosa and lilies, are daily flown to Paris and even London through the winter months. Many plantations are equipped with demountable greenhouses to cover their roses, so that December and January blooms, fetching a high price, can be forced. But even without such protection the rose season is early spring.

Of the smaller towns to stay at in the mountains, within easy motoring distance of the coast, Vence is the best known, a clean, bright, open place with a handsome *place*, excellent restaurants and hotels, all rather dear. Many of the villages, however—Tourettes is an example—are delightful, and have good, small inns and *pensions*. Tourettes is a quaint place of ancient stone houses and very narrow cobbled streets, magnificently sited on the lip of a gorge, with a sheer precipitous hillside falling far to a fertile valley. Such siting is not at all unusual in these mountains, for it made the villages and settlements easy to defend, so that fine views are two a penny in many of the villages. And the surroundings are exciting—crags and scarps, torrential rivers, waterfalls, noisy trout-streams. Some of the highest villages, strongly fortified still—for the fortifications have easily outlasted the people—are abandoned, eerie places to visit in the mountain mists, reached by roads dangerous to any but the most experienced drivers. The whole of this country was much fought over for centuries: at one time the enemy was the Moors, who held part of it for considerable lengths of time. Various kinds of North African pirates, as well as the official forces of Islamic powers, raided the coast and penetrated the hills. Provence was frequently at war with France: and I have already mentioned the Manichean heresy outbreak which was only put down by one of the cruellest of the many cruel religious wars of the Middle Ages. Hence the fortification of the mountain villages, and their dramatic siting.

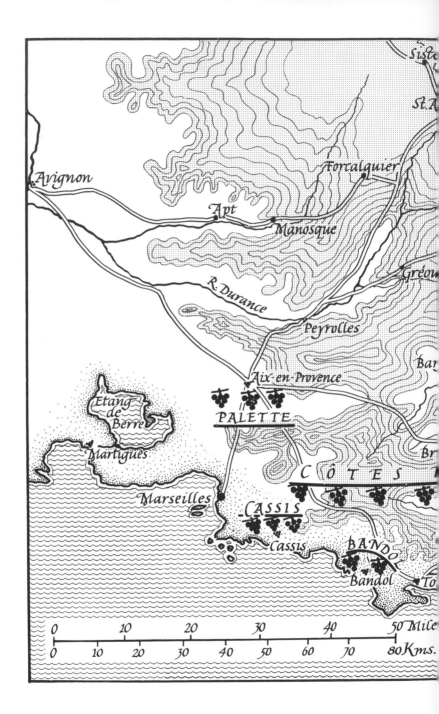

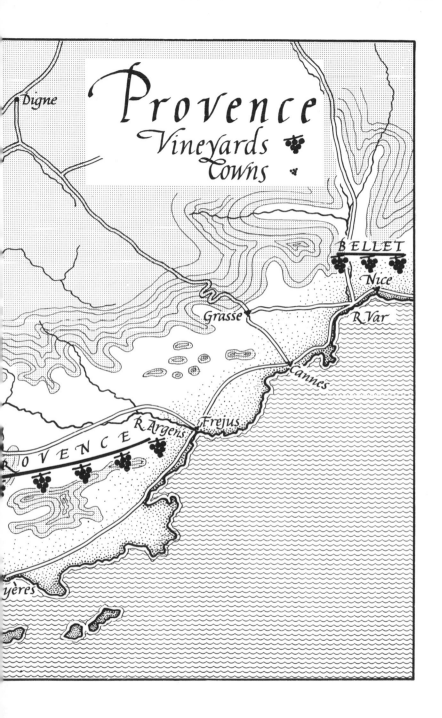

Digne

Provence
Vineyards
Towns

BELLET

Nice

Grasse

R. Var

Cannes

R. Argens

Frejus

ROVENCE

yères

As for wine, as I have said, the *département* affords only one vintage of distinction, Bellet. But there are other vineyards for both wine and table grapes, and although much of this ordinary wine is poor, some of it is by no means bad, perfectly adequate for ordinary daily drinking, and can be bought from the wood at village *débits de vin*.

Inland, and rising steeply from this region, there are two wine-growing places in the *Hautes-Alpes*, one about Gap and known as the Gapenais; the other about Embrun, and known as the Embrunais. Here the land is all between 3,000 and 10,000 feet above sea-level, which is rather high for wine-growing even at latitude 45°. The vineyards, however, are in the *Haute Vallée de la Durance*, the Upper Durance valley, itself averaging 3,300 feet above sea-level, but backed to the north by land rising over 9,000 feet, and still farther north, to over 13,000 feet; to the north-east are the Cotiennes. Thus the valley is sheltered from the coldest quarters. Moreover, the vines are planted on very steep, south-facing slopes—some of them so steep, indeed, that the workers, hoeing or pruning or gathering the harvest of grapes, have to be roped like mountaineers. Some of the vines cultivated, apart from such well-known varieties as Aramon and Cinsaut, are entirely local *cépages* of considerable antiquity, such are the Mollard vine, also known as Taillardier and Chaliant, a variety valued for its great resistance to fungus diseases and yielding a quite good *vin ordinaire*; and Téoulier, sometimes called Plant du Four or, after a region farther south, Manosquen, whose wine has rather more character than Mollard.

At this point in the viticultural tour we are not far from a region already visited, for Savoy lies just to the north. It will be necessary to turn about, and the pleasantest return will be by way of the mountain roads, through magnificent country of dramatic panoramas, by way of Barcelonette, Seyne, Digne, Sisteron, Manosque, following the Durance valley; then Salon, Arles, Lunel and Montpellier, as an appropriate centre for the Languedoc vineyards, for Montpellier is the academic capital of viticulture where, at a branch of the University devoted to the vine, the subject is under constant research-study. There, too, is a vineyard of hundreds of varieties, the most complete collection of its kind in the world. It was from this collection that in 1823 James Busby took cuttings of 437 varieties which he carried with him to Australia for trial and selection, so that it was in Montpellier that the growing Australian wine industry began.

The wine-growing of Languedoc is so important that it dominates the economy of three *départements*, Gard, Hérault and Aude, which have, respectively, 180,000, 360,000 and 240,000 acres of vines cultivated by 160,000 *viticulteurs*, some of them single-handed smallholders, others very large firms using a great deal of machinery and employing much labour.

CARCASSONNE AND THE BAS-LANGUEDOC

If, in making your way west, you start at Beaucaire and take a side road whose number I forget, to Nîmes—where the Maison Carée, now a museum but formerly a Greek temple and almost perfectly preserved as such, is well worth visiting—if you then drop down by the main road through Lunel and Montpellier, and thereafter take the road through Mèze, on one of the lagoons, Pézénas in the Herault, Béziers and Narbonne; and if, finally, from Narbonne you go on to skirt the Corbières hills—virtually the foothills of the Pyrenees—and drive on to Carcassonne, you will have driven completely through the vine-plains of Lower Languedoc. These constitute one of the three regions into which the south-eastern vineyard of France is divided, and they include the plains of Beaucaire, the littoral of the Gard and Herault *départements*, the plains of Montpellier, the Bitterois and the Narbonnais.

Excepting for the fringes of the lagoons, with their peculiar flora and fauna, the salt marshes and the white, sunblasted towns, it is not interesting country. But from the point of view of the ordinary Frenchman-in-the-street, in the lower-income bracket, as the phrase is, by which is meant the poor, it is very important country indeed, for it produces a large part of the ordinary wine drunk by most French people at least twice a day at their meals. The Gard and the Herault alone produce 14,500,000 hectolitres of wine annually, which is about 426,000,000 bottles—enough to keep every family in France supplied for three weeks.

The visitor cannot conveniently visit the three divisions of Languedoc wine country in what I will call oenological order, because the grouping in classes of wine is not geographical but geological. Roughly, the three kinds of wine are wines of the plains, wines of the hills and wines of the mountains. And whereas some of the hill wines are on the extreme east of the great plain vineyards, others are north, or west, of it. I shall stick to the oenological order, for it will be easy for the reader to make his own route by reference to the map.

But first, as to a centre at which to stay: the choice is wide. Béziers and Narbonne are central, but they are towns of which I know too little to say anything. Carcassonne is too far to the west, but otherwise attractive; for excepting only Williamsburg, in Virginia, it is perhaps the only town in the world which is a complete museum-piece. The people of this walled, medieval fortress-town do not, it is true, make themselves ridiculous by going about their work in doublet and hose, wimple and stomacher, helmets and plate armour, as the people of Williamsburg serve behind the counters of their shops in the appropriate fancy-dress. Carcassonne has at least some modern life of its own, it is not quite a fossil. Two of its hotels are of extraordinary magnificence. My wife and I once dined alone in the dining-room of one which is a vast, medieval hall, its dark panelling decorated with glowing coats-of-arms, and its tall, narrow windows casting down great solid-looking beams of coloured light. And in early spring, the plain out of which the city seems to spring like a great tree when you approach it from the north or east, is glorious with wild flowers, notably an enchanting dwarf blue iris which I never identified, although I recall it as some kind of *I. reticulata*.

The Bas-Languedoc plain wines have nothing to recommend them but soundness. The wine economy of the region is interesting as an example of the great importance of smallholding in this industry, even where large-scale machine cultivation is the rule. In the Gard, for example, half the total area under vines is in holdings of less than six acres; and in the Hérault, no less than 69 per cent of the vineyards are in this category. Only 10 per cent of the Gard holdings are over 30 acres, and only 3 per cent of the Hérault vineyards. But this 3 per cent of the total *number* of holdings represents 30 per cent of the total area planted to vines in the *département*, while in the Gard the 10 per cent of the number of holdings over 30 acres represents 55 per cent of the whole Gard plain vineyard. In other words, there are numerous very small holdings, many under one acre; and a very few enormous properties worked on 'industrial' lines.

Obviously, although the independent peasant cultivators can, by very hard work, compete against the big companies in growing grapes (the experience of family-holdings in France, Denmark and Holland, in various branches of horticulture, shows that manual work and intensive methods are far more efficient in terms of yield-per-acre than industrialized holdings), they could not, as individual or family businesses, compete when it comes to making the wine. There are very great economic advantages in large-scale pressing machinery, and generally in making and handling wine in great bulk, although there are grave oenological disadvantages. (In the case of fine wines, it is probable that the optimum size of a cask, for instance, is 50 gallons.) But then in the Languedoc plains there can be no question of a *grand vin*, which can be made only at the vineyard with careful personal attention. To compete with the great firms, therefore, or sometimes as a form of alliance with them, the growers are organized by themselves into cooperatives, which take their grapes, make and sell the wine and distribute the profits.

As to the *cépages* of these plains, about 45 per cent of all the vines planted are Aramon; a quarter are Carignan. Both are typical southern varieties. Colour is given to the reds, which predominate, of course, as always in hot-country wines, by about 10 per cent of *teinturiers* grapes, with red juice. There are also some thousands of acres of PD varieties. And, in the Hérault, an old and still good variety called Terret-Bourret. Finally, Clairette, which is not now a Bordeaux variety but from which comes our name for the red Bordeaux wines, claret.

So much for the wines of the Bas-Languedoc plains. They are not distinguished and they have no pretensions; but they are very far from negligible, for they are the support of several hundred thousand French families and the daily drink of millions.

The Slopes and Plateaux

The hillside and plateaux vineyards of Languedoc, producing rather better wine than the plains, are several. Listing them from east to west, they are:

(a) Clairette de Bellegarde, Bellegarde being a town half-way between Nîmes and Arles.
(b) Cotières du Gard, just south of Nîmes.
(c) Clairette du Languedoc, grown in the Soubergues de l'Hérault, on the middle reaches of that river.
(d) Minervois. The vineyard is on the lower slopes of the steeply rising arc of foothills which begins north of Carcassonne and sweeps round to a point south of St. Pons, a town which stands at 200-odd feet above sea-level. The wines of Minervois are therefore true hill-wines.
(e) Frontignan. About the town of that name.
(f) Blanquette de Limoux. Limoux is a town south of Arles at about 1,000 feet in the foothills of the Pyrenees. Its people, although politically French, are culturally Catalan.

In point of quantity, the principal wines produced by all the above vineyards are *vins de consommation courante,* as useful and as wanting in character as the wines of the plains. But in addition, some wines of superior quality are grown and made, wines of some interest, and which, for our own purposes, I will separate into two groups regardless of geography. The table wines, which are better than the plain wines by reason of altitude and poor soil of the vineyard site, and dessert wines—sweet wines of enormous alcoholic strength which owe their character to the extremely hot and sunny sites on which they are grown, to the varieties of the vines which yield them, and to carefully controlled techniques of vinification and 'fortification'.

The superior wines of the *plateaux* and *coteaux* are officially graded into two classes, VAOC—*vins d'appellation d'origine controllée*—and VDQS.

In the first, higher class, there are five wines of particular interest or worth. The white Clairette de Bellegarde is substantial, golden, fruity and rich; and very similar to it is the second, Clairette du Languedoc, made from grapes harvested on the slopes of the middle Hérault valley, amidst some very beautiful river scenery. The red wines of Fitou are much better than the reds of the plains, and excellent to drink in moderate quantity with the highly spiced meat dishes typical of the Languedoc and Catalan *cuisine*. The other two to be noted are the *vins doux naturels* —VDN—and *vins de liqueur*—VDL—of Frontignan and Lunel, made exclusively from muscat grapes. These after-dinner wines are very sweet (some are less so than others), very strong in alcohol and richly fragrant and flavoursome with the delicious taste of muscat grapes. As Roussillon also produces wine of this kind—and in my opinion still better —some of it relatively 'dry', this will be a good point to explain the nature of VDN, which is by no means 'natural', despire its name; and VDL. The making of both is laid down in detail by French wine law, and must be strictly adhered to if the *Appellation* is to be used in selling the wines.

You will frequently see it stated that the sweet wines of the Bas-Languedoc and the Roussillon are so vinted as to have more than 20 per cent, or 20°, alcohol. This gives many people the false idea that this alcohol is naturally produced in the course of ordinary fermentation. This is not so; in fact it is impossible. It is just possible that there are some local yeast strains in some parts of France which will produce 17° of alcohol before they stop work, even if plenty of sugar remains in the wine. As a rule, 15° is about the top figure. But 24°, which is the kind of figure we are dealing with here, is out of the question, there is no yeast known to biology that will produce so much, and no reason to suppose that such a yeast exists. In short, the Frontignan, Lunel, Banyuls and other sweet and liqueur wines are, like port and sherry, although in a different fashion, fortified with spirit, the quantities added being calculated in terms of 100 per cent pure alcohol, although actually added in the form of 90°—the 'degree' in question being, for those who are interested, the standard Guy-Lussac measurement. So that it is as well to remember that although a smallish glass of Frontignan or Lunel is pleasant with a dish of nuts, or with confectionery or pastries, if you drink any more you had better watch your temper the next morning.

A VDN has to be made as follows: the *must* has to be of Muscat, Grénache, Maccabeo or Malvoisie grapes; either all, or some, or just one, according to the wine in question. In the case of one or two *Appellations* it is permissible to use, as to one-tenth of the total *must* by volume, some other *cépages*. The natural sugar content of this *must*, measured by refractometer or a specific-gravity hydrometer, has to be such that it would produce 14° of alcohol by ordinary fermentation, that is, about the maximum any good yeast can be expected to yield when one is not trying to break records. In the *course of fermentation,* i.e. *not* after the wine is made, alcohol equal to between 5 and 10 per cent of the volume of the *must,* is added to it. This has to be done a bit at a time, so as not to stop fermentation, but it will finally do just that, when plenty of sugar still remains in the wine, at which point the alcoholic strength may be about 20°. The amount of sugar remaining is not laid down by law in the case of VDN wines, hence their diversity in this respect.

A VDL wine is made as follows: once again the *must* has to be composed of specified *cépages*, often muscat, but there are several others. The alcohol is added before and during fermentation, which is thus under control all the time, and it is done in such a way that fermentation stops when, (*a*) 15° of alcohol has been added to the wine and (*b*) a stated quantity of sugar still remains unconsumed. Where the *must* is of muscat grapes, the amount of sugar has to be 178 grammes per litre. Where the *cépage* is Pineau des Charentes, the sugar content is 170 grammes per litre. But there are special figures for the VDL wines of the lower Roussillon, in which case the total of alcohol added to the wine is no less than 21·5°, the natural alcohol only about 5°, and almost all the natural sugar is thus conserved. Such a wine is a sort of highly intoxicating jam.

* * * * * *

To return to the wines of the *plateaux* and *coteaux*: the last of interest is Blanquette de Limoux, which is, as far as I know, the only sparkling wine of the region, and which is derived exclusively from the very sugary little grapes of Mauzac vines, so that it is both alcoholic and sweet. That completes the list of *Appellation Controllée* wines.

The VDQS wines are: Cotières du Gard, Coteaux de St. Christol, St. Drezery, St. Georges d'Orques, St. Chinian, Licpoul de Pinet, all in the Hérault. Quatourze, La Clape, Corbières and Corbières Supérieures in the Aude; and, straddling Hérault and Aude, Minervois.

The mountain wines of Languedoc are of no importance, presumably because nobody has ever concentrated on improving them, for there are conditions which should be suitable for the production of good wine. The vineyards in the subsistence-plus-cash-crops smallholdings of the foot-hill country where the Cevennes mountains begin, are all very small, part of somebody's little farm or market-garden. Most of the vines are PD, and unfortunately they are usually of the older, 'foxy' varieties. What is even more lamentable, quite a number of the peasants are still growing varieties which are categorically forbidden by law, neither viniferas nor French-bred hybrids, but strains of American species, notably *V. labrusca*, for instance the variety Clinton, which yield wine, indeed, but very nasty wine. Several times, when motoring slowly through these happily remote and tranquil mountains, whose valleys are, in May and June, fragrant and lovely with endless drifts of wild nar-cissus, aquilegia and orchids, I have had my big two-litre Tuscan bottle filled with a khaki-coloured turgid fluid made from Clinton or Noah grapes, and more or less undrinkable. The Cevennes mountaineers are an austere, chestnut-eating, Calvinist people; it is possible that they regard good wine as a wicked indulgence.

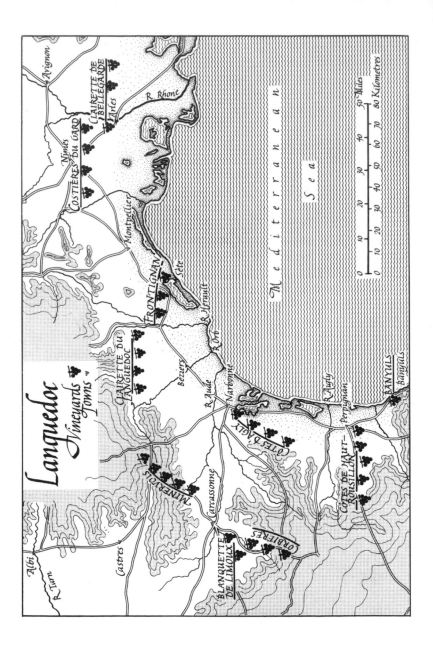

Roussillon

I can never make out whether the wines of Agny belong to Languedoc or to the Roussillon. The slopes where they are grown are on the lower hills of the Corbières mountains, in the Aude *département*, facing almost due east and extending between a point west of Fitou and a point south of Narbonne. Fitou has a red wine with its own *Appellation*, and it is the only one I know from these *Côtes*. The coast beyond is of particular interest for the waders and diving birds which frequent the coastal lagoons.

The *département* called Pyrénées-Orientales, in the Roussillon, is the extreme south-east province of France, having frontiers with both Spain and the Republic of Andorra. The wine slopes of the Corbières mountains extend from south of Limoux to somewhere north-west of Tarascon in the valley of the Ariège—not to be confused with Tartarin's Tarascon in the Rhône valley. Tarascon, like Limoux, is a Catalan town, and the French spoken there is a *patois* not easy to follow. I dare say that most people, when at school, heard the expression *parler français comme une vache espagnole* which, although doubtless amusing, is meaningless: it is probably a corruption of *parler français comme un basque espagnol*. Well, the Tarasconais of the Ariège valley are Catalan French, but they speak French like their westerly neighbours, the Basques. Tarascon being well above the 3,000-feet contour, the Corbières wines are true mountain wines.

Next to these slopes and well to the south of Perpignan are the *Côtes de Haut-Roussillon*, with several wines of some distinction which we will come to in a minute. And, finally, Roussillon wines include those made right down on the coast near to the Spanish frontier, by Port Vendres: the wines of Banyuls.

Roussillon is a relatively insignificant province from the oenological point of view. For the most part mountainous, and with a fine, still not too crowded coast in places precipitous, and provided with ancient fishing villages, its interests are in grazing, sheep, goats, some industry, smuggling on a considerable scale, and fishing. The typical fishing port, and a good place to stay, is Collioure. Not that it is by any means 'undiscovered': it is unhappily long past the stage of being the *petit coin pas cher* which French intellectual holiday-makers and their English copyists are always hoping to find. But it is relatively unspoilt, not over exploited. Its fishermen still really fish, but its hotels and restaurants are more or less sophisticated.

All the eating-places of this coast make a great fuss about their *bouillabaise*, the famous saffron stew of diverse kinds of fish. Mediterranean fish is, by the high standards set by the English Channel and the North Sea, coarse and flavourless, and very good, very high-flavoured cooking is necessary to make it edible. Fortunately, Roussillon cooking *is* good, which fact, combined with the cheapness and quality of the local wines and the pleasures of admirable swimming beaches, makes places like Collioure crowded in summer.

The bulk of the Roussillon wines are grown on the alluvial plain about Perpignan, a dusty and curiously melancholy town even in bright sunshine. They are sound, ordinary wines, very adequate for daily drinking; but it is not necessary to drink them, for superior in quality and interest are the local VDQS wines, Roussillon Dels Aspres, and the Roussillon Corbières and Corbières Supérieures.

The wines for which the province is famous, however, are its *vins doux naturels* and its *vins de liqueur*, which are made in the manner described for Frontignan and Lunel in the Languedoc. The place-names involved are Banyuls, Maury, Rivesaltes, the Haut-Roussillon *côtes*, and the *Côtes d'Agly*. All these wines are entitled to the *Appellation, Grand Roussillon*. In Frontignan the principal *cépage* for sweet wines is Muscat; and in the Roussillon it is Grénache, with Muscat, Malvoisie and Maccabeo as auxiliary varieties. The best vineyards are narrow terraces either overlooking the sea and fully exposed to the sun all day long or similar terraces overlooking the coastal strip from the Pyrenean foothills. The yield per acre is the lowest in France, 200 gallons, that is about 1,200 bottles. There are several reasons for this, but the predominant one is that grapes selected for the very highest sugar content and strong flavour are not very good for wine-making, since they are not juicy but pulpy. Their yield in juice is low; but the sugar in that juice may be as much as 30 per cent of the whole by volume. However, there are enough of these low-yielding terraces to make up an annual total of 4,000,000 gallons of sweet wines, so that the industry is important to the province and the wines are drunk all over France, though I do not recall ever seeing any in England.

Altogether there are some 136,000 acres of Roussillon under vines, belonging to and worked by 31,000 *viti-culteurs,* most of them smallholders relying on the family for labour, but with some large firms.

A final point: not all VDN and VDL wines are white or yellow, although those are probably the best. About three-fifths of the total Roussillon production of sweet wines are whites, the rest are reds and *rosés.* In the case of wines of this kind the colour has no significance for the character and taste, however—or very little.

CHAPTER ELEVEN

CORSICA

THE island of Corsica is best known to the English not as a vineyard but as a breeding-ground for bandits. Its bandits, if any remain, were never altogether mere bandits, but a sort of amateur nationalists determined to maintain old Corsican customs which conflicted with French law and order. There was, as in Sicily, a touch of politics in their banditry. It is always difficult to draw a line between political irredentism and robbery-with-violence. If successful on a really magnificent scale, as in the case of Napoleon Bonaparte, the most distinguished of Corsicans, international robbery-with-violence becomes a respectable political operation and as such is loudly praised by historians. But since Napoleon's day the Corsicans have given up providing France with magnificent robbers, and have provided her with coppers instead: a surprising number of high-ranking men in the French police are Corsicans; just as a surprising number of New York policemen are Irish.

The principal reason for criminal outlawry in Corsica— all this has nothing whatever to do with grape-vines and wine—is the blood-feud. Corsicans, being hostile to the French police in their own island, tend to gang up against them when they are in pursuit of a man who has killed in a blood-feud. And the existence of the *maquis*, the wild, mountainous and jungly hinterland of the island in which a wanted man can take refuge, makes it very difficult for the police to lay hands on him. Respect for the blood-feud means that a man may be forced to kill 'for honour'. But the French police take the doubtless narrow-minded view that a man who kills for honour is as much a murderer as a man who kills for money. The so-called 'bandits', then, are simply outlaws who have taken to the *maquis* after avenging a family wrong. As I say, this kind of thing may be no more in the island.

But when I was first there twenty-five years ago these *mores* were still general. I have heard that Corsican manners have lately become more mild and conciliating. Probably they have: it is a curious fact that the uglier and more brutal and ruthless public violence—warfare and police action—become, the milder does private violence become. But in any case, visitors may go to Corsica now, as always in the past, without fear of being involved in a shooting affray. Corsicans have always been remarkable for courtesy; they have, and their history and literature is full of it, that quality of elegant civility and affability in dealing with strangers, of considerate *gravitas*, which is delightful to the sensitive foreigner.

The island is one of the most beautiful in the world. It is a solid lump of very diverse and interesting mountains with a narrow coastal strip of lowlands: it is still, in parts, well wooded, with deciduous hardwoods at the lower altitudes and pines above. The coast is dramatic, there is good swimming, fishing and even shooting. The littoral, and the plateaux and valleys of the interior, provide good, fertile soils for wheat and other crops, and there is much pasture of herds and flocks. The large and very handsome native asses still provide a good deal of the transport in the interior for men and freight. The principal crop of the island is olive oil. For, like the vine, the fig and the almond, the olive will do very well on thin soils overlying rock, and so enables people with an 'ungrateful' soil to exploit it. It was on this foundation that the greatness of Athens was built; and the olive has been a good friend to the Corsicans. Other fruits also flourish there, not only the fig and the almond and the grape but the lemon. Considerable quantities of lemons are exported; and Corsica is the only place in Europe where I have eaten sweet lemons, although no doubt they do grow elsewhere. Peaches do well, and oranges; at higher latitudes, pears and apples. Bougainvillea is happier there than in the South of France, and in spring the island is famous for the great profusion of its flowers, both wild and cultivated. There are numerous species peculiar or at least native to Corsica, among them the very handsome *Rosemarinus corsicans*, the rosemary with dark blue flowers.

The people are of mixed stock, but their manners and *patois* are more or less Italian. French is spoken, at least on the coast, as a second language, like English in Welsh Wales: in the interior one finds villages where French is not of much use to one.

Although there are small vineyards almost everywhere in Corsica, for many smallholders make their own wine and sell the surplus locally, the commercial viticultural regions are well marked: they are Sartène; Cap Corse with Calvi and Calenzana; Patrimonio; and Ajaccio.

Sartène is a small mountain town in the southern half of the island, at about 1,500 feet above sea-level. It is about thirty miles by the coastal and mountain main road from Bonifacio, the southernmost port of the island; and above fifty miles by a magnificently 'scenic' main road from Ajaccio, the big west-coast port; the road is almost entirely engineered through the mountains, and crosses the river Tarave at Petreto, which as far as I can recall is the only town on the whole route. The wines of Sartène are both white and red, full-bodied, well-balanced and usually in excess of 12° alcohol.

Cap Corse is the only Corsican wine which is widely known, exported in considerable quantities to France and, in small, occasional consignments, to England. It will throw some light on the nature of this heavy, red, sweet wine if I confess that at one time I thought there was a connection between the name *Corse* and the adjective *corsé*, which is invariably used of any full-bodied wine (and also to imply stoutness, strength, substance in things other than wine). Actually *corsé* is the past-participle of the verb *corser*, which means to give body, volume, substance, flavour, to something, and it presumably comes from the same root as *corps*. At all events, the wine principally known as Cap Corse, although not the only one grown in that vicinity, is a heavy red apéritif or dessert wine very strong

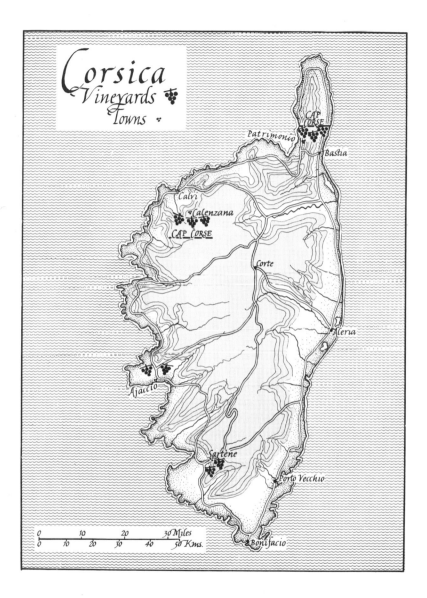

Corsica
Vineyards 🍇
Towns ❧

CAP
CORSE

Patrimonio

Bastia

Calvi

Calenzana

CAP CORSE

Corte

Aleria

Ajaccio

Sartène

Porto Vecchio

0   10   20   30 Miles
0   10   20   30   40   50 Kms.

Bonifacio

in alcohol and which you can drink as you would port or brown sherry, madeira or marsala.

Cap Corse, the place, is the northernmost cape of Corsica, the tip of the peninsula which sticks out like a handle. This piece of land is an oval cone, having a coastal strip of lowland but rising regularly all round to a ridge or hog's back of mountains of about 3,000 feet. It is not, unless a road has been built quite recently, particularly accessible, for the main road ends—or used to end until a few years ago—at Bastia on the east coast at the root of the peninsula, and at St. Florent on the gulf of that name in the west. Some of the Cap Corse wine is grown in the peninsular vineyards, and some to the south-west in vineyards which lie between Calvi and Ile Rousse.

The wines of Ajaccio and Patrimonio are not like Cap Corse, but are table wines, dry and rather 'hard'. They are grown in terrace and plateau vineyards, those of Ajaccio, the principal jumping-off place in Corsica for tourists, on the slopes to the north and east of the town where the land begins to rise towards the 200-metre contour.

Corsican table wines, while they are perfectly sound, have no character of subtlety or delicacy. As is always the case where the conditions are far from ideal—and Corsica is far too hot a country to produce really fine wine—a very great deal depends on the skill and conscience of the vintner. Where vinification is well done, both red and white wines are very good, quite well balanced and pleasant drinking at four or five years. Where vinification has been careless, the reds are harsh and the whites want clearness.

All the vineyards in Corsica, private and commercial, do not amount to 20,000 acres, of which about 16,000 are commercial plantations. These are planted in part to ancient, local *cépages* which cannot be identified with any mainland varieties; and to others which, although they have Corsican names, are not particularly Corsican, and can be identified as well-known French or Italian varieties. Thus the Macalu of Ajaccio and Sartène, the Vermentino of Calvi and elsewhere (it is also called Garbesso), are in fact Mourvedre and Malvoisie respectively, although the Malvoisie strain of the Corsican vineyards is the Favorita of Italy. White wines are made from the grapes of Rossola bianca, which is the Ugni blanc of the mainland. Between 1945 and 1950 there were new plantations made with newly introduced varieties, Cinsaut and Grenache, the latter presumably with a view to making a new *vin doux naturel*, or improving Cap Corse.

To recommend Corsica simply for its wines would be exaggerating. But there are fifty other reasons for going there—its fine old towns, curious churches of mixed styles and periods, splendid mountains, glorious coast, its flowers, its people, its relatively empty interior, its singular fossilized political cult of Bonaparte. And for whatever reason you go, there is no need at all to be thirsty, for though Corsican wines may not be very distinguished, they make wholesome drinking.

CHAPTER TWELVE

JURANÇON AND THE SOUTH-WESTERN WINES

THIS swift circular tour of French wines began on the Garonne, and being circular must end in the same neighbourhood. To complete the circle we want wines grown west of Roussillon and south of Armagnac. We find them in ancient Navarre; west of the source of the Garonne in the Pyrenees, both the *Hautes-Pyrénées-et-Basses-Pyrénées départements*; in the *Lot* and the *Tarn, Lot-et-Garonne* and *Tarn-et-Garonne*.

This region, one of mountains falling to rich plains and alluvial valleys, is yet another of the diversities of France. The heart of France, what we might call French France, is the Touraine, and it has its own golden wines. But, as we have seen, the most notable of the vineyards are in the peripheral provinces; often, as it were, in un-French France. True, Bordeaux, the most important, is French enough, and so is Champagne. But Burgundy has its own kind of foreignness, Jura a Swiss flavour, Alsace is Franco-German, the Languedoc is far in spirit from the clear Gallic cheerfulness. Roussillon is Catalan. And Navarre, the last of the series, is Basque.

It will be recalled that Navarre was not joined to France until its king, Henry, became Henri Quatre of France and Navarre. At that time Navarre was Protestant—or at least its royal family was—and Henry's cynical conversion—*Paris is worth a mass*—was the price paid for union. The king, by his favour, made at least one of the Navarre wines famous: Jurançon, one of the most distinguished of mountain wines, which is topaz in colour and has a musky flavour and a bouquet of truffles which gives it a character all its own.

The Basques are rather a mysterious folk. The demo-graphic history of Europe is one of invading hordes from the north and east driving the peoples they found in possession back to the periphery of the continent, or of the land in question. Probably the ancient inhabitants of Europe, at all events of France, were forced out of the pleasant and fertile plains and valleys of the interior by the invading Celtic peoples, just as the Celts themselves were, to some extent in France and altogether in Britain, forced out to the leaner lands by invading Teutons. It is at least possible that the Basques are a vestige of a still earlier 'refugee' race, forced to take to the mountains by the all-conquering Gauls. It is certain that they are not Gallic and that they are a peculiar people with a marked character of their own. And that they have an extremely ancient, philologically mysterious language connected with no other surviving tongue. In their applied arts, too, they have characteristic, traditional patterns of their own, elaborate and beautiful, and curiously reminiscent of some northern Indian work.

If anyone familiar with the Alps were to be set down suddenly in the Pyrenees, he would not suppose himself in the Alps. I do not know in what the difference consists: mountain scenery is mountain scenery; but there are a thousand small differences which add up to a complete difference. Mountain formations, flora, the air, the quality of the light, all are different. Moreover, the Pyrenees are on the whole less frequented, less overrun, than the Alps. Here, too, once again, is a country of flowers in diversity and profusion, cyclamen and crocus, gentian and narcissus, primula and iris, mountain rose and orchid.

The wines of Navarre and the country joining it to France proper are of three classes: there are *vins de consommation courante*; VDQS; and *vins d'Appellation d'Origine Controllée*. The first, and most plentiful, are grown by the small farmers and smallholders of the local mixed-farming economy. The *cépages* are very diverse: there are varieties from the west such as Picpoul and Meslier St. François; varieties from the Bordelais, such as Cabernet, Malbec, Sémillon and Sauvignon. And there are local and peculiar varieties, Negrette, Valdigne, Mauzac, Ondenc, En de l'El. Finally, the Pyrenean mountain varieties, Tannat, Ruffiat, Gros Mansenc and Petit Mansenc. There are also quite numerous small vineyards of the better hybrids. The co-operative principle does not seem to appeal to the local peasants; at all events, there are few, if any, co-operatives, each farmer making his own wine at the farm, keeping what he will want for his own consumption and selling the surplus, if any. In short the local practice is subsistence viti-culture, the sale of wine being of secondary importance, a pattern which extends well up into the Dordogne country. Of course, there are exceptions—apart from the obvious ones of the *Appellation* and VDQS wines—*Haute-Garonne* favours co-operatives: at Carbonne, for example, there is a very successful co-operative for making and selling the peasant's wine on modern, industrialized lines.

* * * * * *

The VDQS wines of Tarn-et-Garonne, Haute-Garonne, Lot and the Basses-Pyrénées have a growing reputation, and you will drink well anywhere in this country. The wines are very carefully and lovingly vinted, unpretentious but clear and very sound and perhaps the least subject to scientific messing-about of all the wines in France. They are particularly good value for money. In Tarn-et-Garonne, drink Lavilledieu wines; in Haute-Garonne, Fronton and Villan-drie; in the Lot, the wines of Cahors. And while you are in the mountains proper, at least in the Basses-Pyrénées *département*, you should try three wines, Rousselet de Béarn, *rosé* de Béarn and Irouléguy.

Still better, dearer (but still cheap), are the AOC wines of the south-west. Beginning in the extreme south with the moun-tain wines, Madiran has a very good white made from Sémillon and Sauvignon grapes, and a good red derived from the local Tannat *cépage*. The best locally famous *cru* of Madiran is Pacherenc du Vic Bilh, a Basque name, like Irouléguy. There are, I think, only two Jurançons, a red made from Bouchy grapes which is good; and the topaz, from Ruffiat and Mansenc grapes, which is excellent, though peculiar, and which I have already mentioned as Henri Quatre's favourite.

Moving north we come to the wines of the Tarn. Incidentally, the road which follows the course of that turbulent river through the part known as the Gorges du Tarn, is scenically one of the most exciting in France. The gorges are deep, narrow and winding, the river crashes and foams over a bed of boulders. There are rapids and waterfalls and, if you go in spring, not many tourists. In May we found a tiny, salmon-pink primula which grew in great clusters, rooted in clefts of water-drenched rock. The road is such that admiring the view and driving should not be combined.

The Tarn *Appellation* wine is called Gaillac; there are actually two Gaillacs, both white and both made from Mauzac grapes, locally pronounced Moissac, or known by a synonym—*Blanquette sucrée*. One wine is still and very good; the other is sparkling and probably good of its kind. The still Gaillac is substantial for a white wine, fruity and rather heady.

Linking up with our point of departure, and completing the circular tour, there are the AOC wines of *Lot-et-Garonne,* and the *Dordogne départements*. And these are the best of the south-western wines, comparing well with the fine wines of the Loire, and even with some of the great Bordeaux, although they are not considered as being in the latter class. They are all, as far as I know, made from the grapes of the noblest *cépages,* the varieties cultivated in the great Bordelais vineyards. Nearly all are grown on steep banks above the Dordogne river, on thin soils well exposed to the sun. They are all of much the same character, but outstanding are the *crus* of Bergerac, Rosette and the Côtes de Duras. And these lead up to the two crowning growths of the region; to the magnificent, fruity, golden wine of Montbazillac, already mentioned early in this tour; and the notable reds of Pécharmant, which deserve to be so much better known than they are.

Being, with these *crus,* back where we started, almost in the Armagnac where Picpoul vines in silica-clays yield the wine from which the famous brandy is distilled, it will be appropriate to recapitulate a few generalities, summing up what factors they are which go to the making of good wine, whether it be in Bordeaux or Burgundy, Alsace or the Roussillon.

CHAPTER THIRTEEN

THE ELEMENTS OF GOOD WINE

NUMEROUS and diverse though the wines of France be, there are certain more or less ponderable conditions for quality in wine, conditions which have been referred to from time to time in every chapter of this book, which should obtain in every case and every province. In them will be found the reason for the predominance of France in viticulture and oenology. Although Italy has more acres under vines than France, France produces more wine, and better wines, than any other country in the world. And this is at least in part because, geologically and geographically, the country is 'made for' the job.

The factors which are usually said to make a good wine are three: I believe that the number should be five, and there is something to be said about each of them. Let it be clear that the order in which I have placed them is not an order of precedence; they are so arranged because one must begin somewhere.

Here are the five factors:

Climate   Soil   Variety of the vine
Skill in growing and vinting
The manner in which the above are combined (especially soil and variety)

Climate

In order to grow steadily and healthily, vines need a rainfall in excess of twenty inches a year and are better with about thirty. They also need a certain amount of warmth which may be achieved either by planting below a certain latitude or, in higher latitudes, by planting at a lower altitude or on sites carefully selected for protection from the colder quarters. Winter temperatures are of no importance until we get to places like Siberia, where special precautions may have to be taken or very resistant varieties chosen: most European vines will stand thirty or more degrees of frost when dormant, that is temperatures which are rare in the temperate parts of Europe. As to the summer and autumn temperatures required, here are the mean monthly figures (ten-year averages) from April to October, the critical months, for four famous wine regions. And since a mean figure can easily mislead—for example, mean *yearly* temperature figures for England give a misleading impression of the summer warmth owing to the mildness of our winters—I also give the ten-year averages for the

Place	April–October mean	August	September
Bordelais (at Bordeaux)	62·57	69	65
Rhine valley	56·43	63	57
Champagne (at Reims)	58·43	65	59
Burgundy (at Dijon)	59·86	66	61

months of August and September separately, since although July and June are important to keep the grapes on the move, these two late summer months determine, to a large extent, the state of ripeness of the grapes at the vintage.

The table is above; the figures in degrees Fahrenheit.

Such figures do not make a lot of sense without another, familiar, set for comparison. On page 194 is a similar table for four places in southern England.

Note the near-equality of Eastbourne and Southampton with the Rhine valley, in point of temperature! Why, then, are not the Sussex and Hampshire coasts planted with

Place	April–October mean	August	September
London (at Greenwich)	55·1	62·6	58
Eastbourne	55·84	61·7	58·4
Southampton	56·43	62·4	58·4
Torquay	56·3	61·2	58·1

vines? The fact is that Alsace is a wine province by virtue of its steep, south-facing slopes, and not of its climate in general. The importance of siting, within this consideration of climate, cannot be exaggerated. But it will occur to some readers that similar favourable sites must here and there be available in south Sussex and in Hampshire, and on the Isle of Wight. They are. There is no doubt whatever that if sites and varieties were chosen by experienced people, southern England could produce good light wines, as it did in the past, on a commercial scale.

Sunshine duration and intensity are generally taken to be implicit in the figures for temperatures. They are not. English and French temperatures are much nearer together than English and French sunshine-hours figures, simply because temperatures can and do remain high under an overcast sky. Only the Atlantic provinces of France have the sort of humidity and cloud normal in England. Now whereas some varieties of grapes will ripen satisfactorily in the requisite temperature more or less regardless of sunshine, others will not. This fact had never been noticed, important though it be, until it emerged from an analysis of the figures for ripening grapes, measured in sugar content at regular intervals, collected for more than a score of varieties by R. Barrington Brock over a period of years, at Oxted, Surrey. It is now, thanks to Mr. Brock's patient and careful research, known that some vine varieties require clear, radiant skies to ripen their fruit; others can make do with sufficiently high temperatures, and with a minimum of direct, unscreened sunshine.

Sunshine-hours to the nearest hour:

Place	April–October mean	August	September
Bordelais	210·3	250	205
Rhine valley	207·3	223	174
Champagne	191.1	197	178
Burgundy	207	242	192

And again, for comparison:

Place	April–October mean	August	September
London (at Kew)	177·7	183	146
Eastbourne	207	223	177
Southampton	186·6	194	162
Torquay	192·1	207	164

Note again that Eastbourne (which, with Sandown, Isle of Wight, is outstandingly sunny above other places in England), has a slightly *more* favourable climate for wine than Alsace, although there is very little between them.

From these small tables it will be obvious that it is a temperate, gently warm climate that produces the most delicate wines, not a hot climate.

The latitudes, in Europe, between which these climatic conditions obtain are 40° N. and 50° N. As for altitude, allowing a variation for latitude, the microclimate is best between 500 feet and 1,000 feet above sea-level. This question of altitude is critical for quality in wine. In Burgundy, for instance, the average altitude for all the *grands vins* vineyards is about 700 feet. The quality of wine declines with quite small differences in the altitude of the vineyards above and below that figure.

Siting is important because the microclimate depends on it: altitude, with clear air-drainage below the site, helps to save vineyards from damage by spring frosts. A strikingly large majority of *grands vins* vineyards are on hillsides or slopes where, in addition to good air-drainage, they get good water drainage and free movement of air, hence lower humidity and greater exposure. It will be found that, as a rule, Burgundian vineyards face south-east or due east—it is the morning sun that is important. Farther north, full south exposure is the rule. In the Bordelais, westerly exposure is not uncommon.

Soil

Vitis vinifera, that is European vines, will grow in any soil whatsoever excepting (*a*) those permanently water-logged and (*b*) very salty soils. The vines grow perfectly well in chalk, but also in acid soil. American species and their hybrids are less accommodating; some are calcifuges. Planting of the new hybrids therefore entails grafting even though *Phylloxera* would not be dangerous to them, because the root must be matched to the soil.

Taking the facts solely from the experience of *grands crus* growers and not from the growers of wine in general, we can say that:

A vineyard ought to be stony. The soils of Château d'Yquem and Château Lafitte are over 60 per cent large stones. In Champagne the best vineyard soils are over 50 per cent large, unbroken lumps of chalk and silex. The great Burgundies are all grown in soils with from 30 to 50 per cent lumps of unbroken rock. White wines are best grown on whitish soils, red on red earths. This is not a case of imitative magic. It is due to the good effects of lime on white wine (see below)—and of iron oxide on red wine. Predominantly silica-sand vineyards tend to yield light wines low in alcohol. In sandy vineyards with no silica, the wine is without bouquet.

Strong clay soils yield wines rich in colour, high in alcohol and tannin, full-bodied and well-balanced. The wines are apt to be harsh when young, but to improve with keeping over long periods. Many, probably a majority, of the great red wines are grown in predominantly clay soils.

Chalk soils yield wines with little body yet highly alcoholic, and with marked bouquet (e.g. the still champagnes).

The action of chalk in emphasizing the fragrances of grapes and bringing them out as bouquet in wine, increases with latitude up to the northern limit. There must be some chemical explanation of this—perhaps calcium is essential to the production of the 'esters' on which these qualities depend—but I cannot find it even in such great pundits as Ribareau Gayon. Humus, above the low limit essential for 'life' in the soil, is pernicious for wine. Soils rich in organic matter yield coarse wines, ill-balanced and apt to spoil or degenerate with keeping.

As we might expect from the above empirical rules, which have emerged from many centuries of experience, the very finest wines are grown in soils containing plenty of stones and gravel, little humus, and which combine clay, silica sands and lime in their composition. These give the wines all the desirable qualities. Thus Romanée-Conti is grown in a soil which is 10 per cent silica sand, 30 per cent clay, 45 per cent chalk but which is amply provided with iron oxide, which gives the wine its rich colour. Clos Vougeot has 47 per cent silica sand, 36·7 per cent clay and 12 per cent chalk, with plenty of iron oxide. The Côte-Rôtie is 86·5 per cent silica sand, 7 per cent clay, 3·2 per cent chalk, and, again, it has enough iron oxide. The differences between one great red wine and another are in large part due to these differences in soil, that is, to the different proportions in which the desirable elements are present.

Variety of Vine

To produce a really fine wine it is essential to (*a*) suit the *cépage* to the climate, and (*b*) suit the *cépage* to the soil. Conservatism in *encépagement* is inevitable because only one *cépage*, or one group of *cépages* whose members are mutually complementary, will produce the qualities associated with the *grand vin* in question.

First, as to matching the variety to the climate, in relatively cold climates it is usual to plant only early, fast-maturing vines. The French group vine varieties in four *époques* by date of ripening the crop, and they break down these *époques* into sub-divisions. Roughly, first epoch varieties are what we would call 'earlies', second epoch 'early mid-season', third epoch 'late mid-season' and fourth epoch 'late'. Within the epoch to which it is attributed a variety will be either *précoce* or *tardif*, so that there are for example early earlies and late earlies. Some first epoch early varieties are what is called *hâtif*, which means that they require only a short season in which to bring their fruit from set to ripeness. These will be planted only where the site is unfavourable, or where latitude makes viticulture marginal, for they are in other respects not very good, and as a rule they are poor croppers. First and second epoch varieties are planted in the principal vineyards south of the Champagne and Alsace regions. Third and fourth epoch varieties are confined to the deep south, for if earlier varieties are grown there the grapes are apt to be overripe for wine, that is, the wine will be seriously short of acid and will therefore taste flat and will not keep.

Thus the matching of varieties to climate is relatively simple, the matching of variety to soil is more complex and entirely empirical. It is a fact that Gamay, growing in the *porphyrique* hillsides of the Beaujolais, produces a fine, delicate, perfectly balanced wine: but that if the same vine be shifted to the chalky marls of Burgundy in identical climatic conditions, the wine is poor, commonplace. Again, Pinot varieties yield fine wines in chalk; coarse, ordinary wines in dense clay. But, just to make it harder, and as an example of the three-way matching which is necessary, for wines of real quality from Pinot a cool climate must be combined with the chalk soil, for in the calcareous clays of the deep south Pinot yields only the coarsest of wine, not only short of acid but with the characteristic taste of Pinots exaggerated to the point of being quite unpleasant.

There is another point here: some varieties, as compared with others growing beside them in the same soil and microclimate, yield wine high in alcohol and low in acid; others wine high in acid and low in alcohol; in other words, given the same soil and the same climate, some grapes are more sugary and less acid than others. And these propensities will be exaggerated in the event of soil or weather being unpropitious to the variety, quite apart from the development of other qualities, characteristic flavour and bouquet. It is possible to detect, in some wines, fine underlying qualities more or less masked, for example by an acidity which renders the wine astringent. Even when the best variety for a given climate-soil complex has been found, it may have inherent faults. The answer in such cases is to grow and blend mutually complementary *cépages*. These may be only two; they may, as in the case of Châteauneuf-du-Pape, be thirteen. More convincing examples of this practice are to be found on the Côte-Rôtie, where the tendency to harshness of the Syrah grape is corrected by a proportion of Viognier grapes in the *must*. In Champagne, Pinot and Chardonnay may be mixed, the proportions varying from year to year. Or, more subtly, and according to the technique devised by Dom Perigord, grapes of the same *cépage* but from different soils and microclimates, that is, from different vineyards, may be mixed to get as near as possible to a perfectly balanced *must*.

Most *grands vins* are derived from a single predominant variety, whose faults may be corrected by small blendings of two or three other varieties. Sometimes no such correction is necessary: the great red Burgundies are pure Pinot. The great red Bordeaux are 85 per cent Cabernet, 10 per cent Merlot and 5 per cent Malbec. The great whites of Sauternes are 75 per cent Sauvignon, 20 per cent Sémillon and 5 per cent Muscadelle.

It is only in the great vineyards that such pains are taken in marrying soil-climate and varieties, and the problem was much complicated by *Phylloxera*, for it became necessary to let in one more 'unknown', the influence of the rootstock on the fruit. The rootstocks, being partly or wholly of American species, have soil requirements which may differ from those of the scion variety. That can be overcome, and has to a large extent been overcome, by breeding new rootstocks to a definite specification, one of the greatest triumphs of horticultural science. But that does not settle the matter: the more bluff-and-bluster school of scientists used to maintain that the rootstock could have no influence on the qualities of the fruit: the character of the scion was fixed by its genetical attributes and that was that. In fact, however, as every grower of apples knows perfectly well from experience, you do not get the same fruit from one stock as from another, though the scion in both cases be from the same twig of the same tree. There can be no doubt at all that the intervention of rootstocks between scion and soil in the case of the great *cépages nobles* of France, has made a difference to the wine. There will soon be nobody alive who has tasted pre-*Phylloxera* vintages, so we shall not be harassed by gloomy old gentlemen telling us that grafting has ruined wine. It has not ruined it; and if it has changed some for the worse, it is reasonable to suppose that it has changed others for the better. Moreover, as progress is made in the science of breeding rootstocks, it may well become possible to correct scion faults by proper choice of stock. In one respect this is already the case; good varieties which produce only small crops can be induced to increase their output by suitable grafting.

Owing to the facts set out above, the certainty that the specific quality of a given wine is due to a given *climate-soil-cépage* complex (and remember that when you buy a wine by name you expect it to have certain attributes and never give a thought to the problem of producing them consistently, although no two years' weather is ever the same), the *Code du vin* chapter of French commercial law has given the force of law to the rules governing the varieties to be grown in each great wine region. For each region a list of varieties is promulgated, and this list has three main heads: recommended *cépages*; authorized *cépages*; tolerated *cépages*.

The Vintner's Skill

Under this head we ought also to include the grower's skill. The quality of grapes produced by a given vine, and on which the quality of the wine depends, does not depend on planting the vine and picking the grapes ten months later. It depends, among other things, on the weight of fruit each vine is allowed to carry, expressed in yield per acre, which means that it depends on the care and thoroughness, as well as skill, of both winter and summer pruning; it depends on what kinds and quantities of manures or fertilizers are used; it depends on prompt and correct control of fungus and insect parasites; it depends on the timing of the vintage.

Skill in vinification is even more important. It entails knowing exactly how to control premature fermentation, how to eliminate undesirable ferments, how to avoid parasites on the yeast, which produce disease in the wine, how to know when, and how much, *chaptelisation* is necessary. The vintner must know how hard and at what speed to press the grapes; when and how often to rack the young wine; the proportions of different varieties of grapes to be used in the particular year, where these are not fixed by rule; what, if any, fining must be done, and how long to keep the wine in wood . . . and a hundred other things.

Vintner and cellarer are helped, like the grower, by scientific advice available at government and co-operative research centres; and by committees of regional experts who issue advice, or even downright orders, at intervals throughout the season which, in French, is appropriately called not the *season* but the *campaign*.

The Fifth Factor

The production of really fine, and even of merely good wine, depends, then, on suitably combining into a working complex, climate, soil, varieties, viticultural skill, oenological skill, and seasonally adaptable judgement on the part of all the people engaged in the job, which skills and judgements are expressions of two not always compatible bodies of knowledge: traditional usage and scientific expertize. And since the whole of this subtle, precariously balanced and very expensive complex can be set at nought by one twenty-minute hailstorm, a fiscal blunder on the part of an official, a change in the bank-rate or a rise in the colossal advertising appropriations from the bloated profits of soft-drink vendors, it is no great wonder that the finest wines are expensive, that good wine is not cheap; and the fact that very adequate wine *is* cheap is, on the other hand, a wonder to be thankful for.

APPENDIX

The 1855 order of merit of Bordeaux wines

RED WINES

Premiers crus

Ch. Lafite

Ch. Margaux

Ch. Latour

Ch. Haut-Brion

Deuxièmes crus

Ch. Mouton-Rothschild

Ch. Rausan-Ségla

Ch. Rausan-Gassies

Ch. Léoville Las Cases

Ch. Léoville Poyferre

Ch. Léoville Barton

Ch. Dufort Vivens

Ch. Gruaud Larose

Ch. Lascombes

Ch. Brane Cantenac

Ch. Pichon Longueville

—Baron de Pichon

Ch. Pichon Longueville

—Comtesse de La-
lande

Ch. Ducru Beaucaillou

Ch. Cos d'Estournel

Ch. Montrose

Troisièmes crus

Ch. Kirwan

Ch. d'Issan

Ch. Lagrange

Ch. Langoa

Ch. Giscours

Ch. Malescot St. Exu-
péry

Ch. Boyd Cantenac

Ch. Cantenac Brown

Ch. Palmer

Ch. Grand La Lagune

Ch. Desmirail

Ch. Calon Ségur

Ch. Ferrière

Ch. Marquis d'Alèsme
Becker

Quatrièmes crus

Ch. Saint Pierre

Ch. Talbot

Ch. Branaire

Ch. Duhart Milon

Ch. Pouget de Chavaille

Ch. La Tour Carnet

Ch. Lafon Rochot

Ch. Beycheville

Ch. Prieurie Lichine

Ch. Marquis de Termes

Cinquièmes crus

Ch. Pontet Canet

Ch. Batailley

Ch. Haut Batailley

Ch. Grand Puy Ducasse

Ch. Grand Puy Lacoste

Ch. Lynch Bages

Ch. Lynch Moussas

Ch. Dauzac

Ch. Mouton d'Armail-
hacq

Ch. du Tertre

Ch. Haut Bages Libéral

Ch. Pedesclaux

Ch. Belgrave

Ch. Camensac

Ch. Cos Labory

Ch. Clerc Milon Mon-
don

Ch. Croizet Bages

Ch. Cantemerle

WHITE WINES

Grand Cru

Ch. d'Yquem

Premiers Crus

Ch. La Tour Blanche

Ch. Lafaurie Peyraguey

Ch. Haut Peyraguey

Ch. Rayne Vigeau

Ch. Suduiraut

Ch. Coutet

Ch. Climens

Ch. Guiraud

Ch. Rieussec

Ch. Rabaud Promis

Ch. Sigalas Rabaud

Deuxièmes crus

Ch. de Myrat

Ch. Doisy Daene

Ch. Doisy Dubroca

Ch. Doisy Védrines

Ch. d'Arche

Ch. d'Arche Lafaurie

Ch. Filhot

Ch. Broustet

Ch. Nairac

Ch. Caillou

Ch. Suau

Ch. de Malle

Ch. Romer

Ch. Lamothe Espagnet

Ch. Lamothe Tissot

INDEX